TRADING WITH ICHIMOKU

T0323019

TRADING WITH ICHIMOKU

A practical guide to low-risk
Ichimoku strategies

Karen Péloille

HARRIMAN HOUSE

HARRIMAN HOUSE LTD

18 College Street

Petersfield

Hampshire

GU31 4AD

GREAT BRITAIN

Tel: +44 (0)1730 233870

Email: enquiries@harriman-house.com

Website: www.harriman-house.com

First published by Maxima, Paris (France). All rights reserved

This English language edition published in Great Britain in 2017

Copyright © Maxima

The right of Karen Péloille to be identified as the author has been asserted in accordance with the Copyright, Design and Patents Act 1988.

Print ISBN: 978-0-85719-615-6

eBook ISBN: 978-0-85719-616-3

British Library Cataloguing in Publication Data

A CIP catalogue record for this book can be obtained from the British Library.

All the charts included in this book have been created on FXCM Trading Station 2.

CONTENTS

ABOUT THE AUTHOR

Karen Péloille has an extensive educational background in Econometrics (statistical and economic modelling) and market finance. She has been trading for her own account since 2008.

Karen specialises in trading with Ichimoku and teaches the principles of this system to professional and private traders in France and in the United States. On top of her trading activities, Karen is a technical analyst and adviser for private clients and portfolio managers.

You may find her technical analysis on her Twitter account: @KarenPeloille

You can contact Karen at karen.peloille@maxima.fr

FOREWORD – BY DAVID LINTON

When I first published *Cloud Charts – Trading Success with the Ichimoku Technique* in early 2010, I had no idea how much interest it would create in the subject. Until then all the works were in Japanese and there was a real lack of solid explanation of Ichimoku charts.

As more and more traders and investors around the world started using Ichimoku, the construction method of these charts became widely available online. Bulletin boards and online forums and chat rooms began to buzz with the latest Ichimoku signal announced here or there. So many of these interpretations regularly seem to be in conflict. The instant gratification that traders often want without properly doing their research or study is concerning and has led to a worrying rise in confusion surrounding using Ichimoku charts.

In this new book on Ichimoku, Karen Péloille takes the reader back to the vital first principles of the technique, clearly covering the importance of each element of the chart construction. Few Ichimoku commentators properly tackle the interpretation of the charts and the author does this admirably in the early chapters of the book. Some new concepts are explored along the way, which is also a welcome new addition to the body of knowledge on Ichimoku charting. It is always nice to see clear examples of how to use Ichimoku and perhaps, more importantly, how not to use it.

The second section on trading gives good practical advice on using Ichimoku for entering and exiting trades and looks in depth at currency pairs where their liquidity lends itself well to using clouds. The following section introduces other techniques to compliment Ichimoku charts in order to arrive at conclusions which concur with this unique method of technical analysis.

The final section on discipline is useful when Ichimoku charts can leave so much to the interpretation of the viewer. It demonstrates the author's practical experience of using the technique on a daily basis and recognises the necessary overrides to have in place when using Ichimoku charts for trading.

I welcome seeing another work on the subject and am confident that *Trading with Ichimoku* by Karen Péloille will be a useful reference in any trader's knowledge base.

David Linton MFTA
CEO Updata
London, 5 June 2017

INTRODUCTION

This book is above all a practical handbook explaining the different elements of the Ichimoku system of chart reading, from the description of each line to their interpretation in a global process of decision-making.

You will rapidly conclude that even though there are only five lines to look at on Ichimoku charts, the information given is very rich and above all complete, more than enough to be able to get both a detailed and global view of the activity of the market and what the price action tells us.

Understanding only the basic reading of this system is enough to be able to trade and be successful.

As a coach for more than five years, I have had the opportunity to meet more than 500 clients, private and professional, eager to learn how to trade with Ichimoku. It's clear to me that the main difficulty which prevents one being successful has little to do with the technical aspect of trading. It's all in the mind. It refers to one's management of emotions, which is harder to master than money management! And, alas, this psychological aspect of trading represents 80% of the success of a trade.

That's why I have included a chapter at the end of this book (Part Four) to explain what trading is from a mental point of view, and why, for example, one can be a fantastic analyst but may never be a good trader. I also try to give some tips to define a kind of road map to train oneself against all the biases induced by the stress of putting money in the market and how to control your emotions in front of the screen.

After reading this book, I hope you will be convinced of the abundance of information you can obtain from these simple five lines and how the Ichimoku method can drastically improve your trading whether you are a beginner or an accomplished trader with a track record below your expectation.

I do not pretend that I have found the Holy Grail but I can assure you that Ichimoku does improve your trading, from the very short-term to long-term time frames.

PART 1

ICHIMOKU THEORY

Introduction

We live in an environment that assumes that the quality of decision-making is directly related to the time and effort spent to gather all necessary information. We believe that the more information that is available to us, the better we will be able to assess the situation and find an appropriate solution. With the ongoing advancement of media, we are overwhelmed with information on a daily basis. This is especially true for the individual who now has access to the same data as professionals. However, we confuse knowledge and understanding, and only the latter can be used to make informed decisions.

So, if you decide to manage your own financial wealth by investing directly in the financial markets and that industry is not your specialty, you will probably start buying countless books and visiting many websites to try to understand all the workings of this 'mysterious' world, so maligned by the mass media. But at the end of all this, will you really *understand* all the information painstakingly collected? I doubt it, because one does not become a financial analyst overnight.

And when you throw yourself into the world of finance, you will undoubtedly follow news events that may impact your investments. Most of the time, the markets will have already anticipated these events and will have priced the information into securities prices. So, your reaction will come too late. In addition, will you really be able to evaluate the impact of the news and its effect on your assets? Keep in mind that the professionals will always be one step ahead of you. For the individual, **this gap between knowledge and analysis of new information means that pure technical analysis (or chartism) gives better results** with less need for learning in the beginning.

Once this fact has been accepted, individuals need to undertake the task of learning technical analysis and selecting the methods they're comfortable with from a long list of tools. Even though they give the illusion of being able to provide all the information necessary to understand the markets, too many technical indicators only represent noise and confusion. Like the saying goes, 'too much information kills information', and we will not be any better prepared to make decisions in the markets.

There's some good news, however: among this range of indicators involving more or less complex calculations, there's one in particular that I discovered in

2009. Once all its subtleties have been explored and all its richness discovered despite its apparent simplicity, one can no longer do without it.

This system is Ichimoku Kinko Hyo, which allows traders to understand market movements with one single glance.

This analysis technique was conceived by Goichi Hosoda (1898–1982), a financial journalist for *Capital Newspaper* in Japan. Being unsatisfied with only interpreting Japanese candlesticks, he added lines to his charts that were similar to moving averages in order to better understand price movements and to detect entry and exit signals in the markets. In the 1930s, he put mathematics students to work in order to manipulate thousands of price data for different stocks in all directions by hand (computers hadn't yet been invented at that time!).

In 1935, he published a first draft of his technique that introduced the Tenkan-Sen under the name 'Ichimoku Sanji'. The first word of this term means 'one glance'.

Despite putting his work on hold during World War II, and after twenty years of tests, he finally published all his research as *Ichimoku Kinko Hyo* in 1968 and described this indicator as we know it today in the seven volumes he wrote.

The three different Japanese characters of this name give all the philosophy of this technical system of analysis:

- *Ichimoku*: 'at a glance' – clarity and rapidity
- *Kinko*: 'equilibrium' – fundamental concept
- *Hyo*: 'chartism'

This overhead view gives perspective and clarity to market research. Charts are simple and information can be immediately interpreted.

However, this method fell into disuse after the death of its author in 1982, and was only revived in 1996 by Hidenobu Sasaki of Nikko Citigroup Securities, who published *Ichimoku Kinko Studies*. This book was voted best technical analysis book by the *Nikkei* newspaper for nine consecutive years. From this, Ichimoku began popping up onto computer screens on trading floors in Japan and later, through American banks' Japanese subsidiaries, in the United States.

As for me, I first discovered this trading system during a conference led by Guido Riolo, EMEA head of technical analysis at Bloomberg, in 2009. It was a revelation as I was struggling with all sorts of different indicators, learning and testing each one without finding the one or the ones that suited me. I only succeeded in appropriating Ichimoku Kinko Hyo's functions in March 2010 when David Linton published his book *Cloud Charts*. I then had the chance to meet an American trader who had used it for two years on a Japanese trading floor and who only uses this indicator when trading.

The Ichimoku Kinko Hyo indicator that I will present to you in this book is therefore the pure system of analysis as conceived by Goichi Hosoda.

The **first part** of the book is devoted to the theoretical description of the various components making up Ichimoku, a necessary step to assess the power of each element. Whatever the technical indicator studied, I consider it essential to understand the mathematical calculation used in order to assess the relevancy of information gleaned from the technical tool.

In the **second part**, I will explain how to trade with Ichimoku Kinko Hyo through several examples in various time frames.

Then, in the **third part**, I will introduce you to different trading methods combining classical tools with Ichimoku Kinko Hyo.

Despite its apparent simplicity, you will discover many subtleties that, thanks to a unique system of validating price movements, make Ichimoku Kinko Hyo an information-rich and extremely reliable trading tool.

1

THEORY

Ichimoku Kinko Hyo is a Japanese term meaning 'equilibrium at a glance'. The most important thing to remember with this indicator is that it depicts **market balance**. The five dynamic lines that make up Ichimoku exemplify price equilibrium points and may be used in markets to signal potential ruptures of such equilibrium.

These lines, analysed as a whole and not separately, provide a perfect overall image of price action at any given moment. One single look at an Ichimoku chart allows us to gauge market sentiment and the strength of the prevailing trend.

This trading system is based on market equilibrium at time t and represents dynamic forces among market participants. A rupture of this equilibrium indicates the taking over of selling or buying interest, which results in prices following a trend. The exhaustion of such a trend gives way to prices stabilising in a new equilibrium until a new rupture takes place. Ichimoku is therefore essentially **a trend indicator**.

Description

Ichimoku charts include five dynamic lines, two of which are in conjunction with actual prices. Two other lines allow us to project past and current market prices into the future. The fifth line provides a representation of market memory.

Throughout this book, I will use the original settings (9, 26, 52) that Ichimoku's founder, Goichi Hosoda, used when developing the indicator. Even if these parameters were originally used in analysis of daily prices, they work suitably in any time frame.

- 9 corresponds with a week and a half of trading sessions (6 + 3)
- 26 is the number of sessions in a trading month in Japan
- 52 = 2 × 26

These settings might be considered inappropriate in today's Western culture given that weeks are made up of five trading sessions and months twenty days. The Forex market is open 24-hours a day. However, changing Ichimoku's settings to 7-21-42 to reflect the functioning of today's markets does not provide us with any more precision and seems even to destabilise the system: interpreting price action becomes more approximate, support and resistance levels are less reliable, and false trading signals more common. Changing the original settings damages Ichimoku's ability to provide a precise glimpse of price action, so much so that even a slightly distorted representation of markets strips the system of its inherent value. Furthermore, it's important to remember that all trading floors (Japanese ones in particular) use the original 9-26-52 settings. It seems like a good idea to use the same information as the professionals and to respect the years of research done by Ichimoku's founder.

Construction

Let's take a look at Ichimoku's construction in detail:

Chart 1.1: Ichimoku

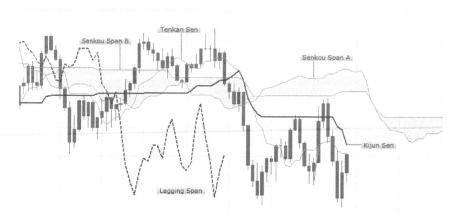

Tenkan Sen (Turning Line – TS)

This line represents the mid-point between the highest high and the lowest low over the last nine periods. Calculating the Tenkan Sen requires identifying the highest high and the lowest low over the last nine candlesticks, adding them all together and then dividing that sum by two. This gives us the mid-point between two extremities over nine periods.

Chart 1.2: Tenkan Sen (Turning Line)

9 Candlesticks

Over time, as new candlesticks appear on the chart, the highs and lows change, resulting in a shift in the mid-point. But if prices remain range-bound without marking fresh highs or lows, this line flattens out and forms a stationary technical level or plateau.

This element is precisely what differentiates Ichimoku's lines with standard moving averages which follow much smoother movements.

Chart 1.3: Tenkan Sen + SMA9

Indeed, the simple moving average (SMA9) in the above chart is calculated by adding up the past nine closing prices and dividing that sum by nine. The notion of plateaus can't exist with the SMA since the resulting calculation will change with every new candlestick that appears.

Plateaus that appear in the Tenkan Sen indicate the absence of a dominating trend or a pause in the most recent trend. Conversely, the steepness of the line's slope provides valuable information regarding momentum and, specifically, alerts during periods in which inflection points in the Tenkan Sen foreshadow weakness in the current trend.

Given that this line follows prices closely due to its short frequency, the market regularly crosses over it without any notable impact on the pursuit of the trend. The main purpose of this line in this system is just to give an alert about the price action. **The Tenkan Sen is the weakest line of all.**

Kijun Sen (Standard Line – KS)

The Kijun Sen is calculated in the same way as the Tenkan Sen and represents the mid-point over the past 26 periods.

Chart 1.4: Kijun Sen (Standard Line)

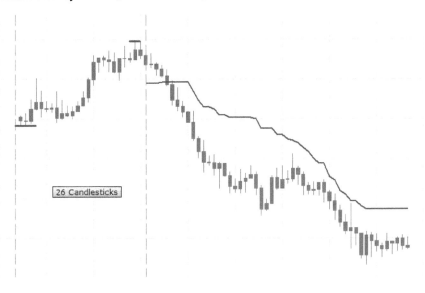

Since the duration taken into account is much longer, plateaus in the Kijun are more pronounced and longer. Because of this, the Kijun provides strong support and resistance levels in the presence of market balance.

A comparison with a 26-period simple moving average (chart 1.5) brings to light the difference between these two types of calculation: as a much smoother line, horizontal levels don't appear.

Chart 1.5: Kijun Sen + SMA26

The information provided by the Kijun is essential to understanding Ichimoku. **It's the main point of reference** for traders who, at first glance, can situate price towards a key support or resistance.

This line, which corresponds to a 50% Fibonacci retracement, plays the role of a magnet in which prices revert to the mid-point once they are too far from it. As we'll see in the chapter dedicated to trading, this is also the line that **gives entry and exit signals in the market**.

The interaction between the Tenkan and the Kijun is of little importance to the overall analysis markets, **crossovers of these two lines not being very significant**. These signals come much too late with respect to the onset of new price movements and can, in the presence of volatility, occur against the trend.

Chart 1.6: Tenkan Sen/Kijun Sen crossovers

To summarise, the Tenkan and Kijun lines represent the **market's pulse**. The Tenkan Sen indicates price volatility and the strength of a given movement through its slope. The Kijun Sen establishes levels upon which equilibrium occurs, thus calling back prices when a state of disequilibrium can no longer sustain itself.

Cloud (Kumo)

The cloud is composed of two lines and is projected in the future (time $t + 26$ periods). **This projection ahead of current market prices** is the first original aspect of Ichimoku, differentiating it with other technical analysis approaches essentially focused on the present.

- The **Senkou Span A (SSA)** is another gauge of market balance because it is calculated by taking the average between the Tenkan and the Kijun, thus giving a representation of price equilibrium between the short term (nine periods) and the medium term (26 periods). This average is then projected 26 periods into the future. Such a projection embodies the cyclical characteristics of price movements: markets have a tendency to return to levels of equilibrium already experienced in the past. Interpretation of the Senkou Span at time *t* gives traders information on support and resistance levels that prices will face 26 periods from the present.

Chart 1.7: Senkou Span A (SSA)

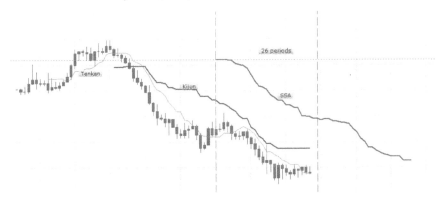

- The **Senkou Span B (SSB)** is the second line making up the cloud. It's also an important measure of market equilibrium due to its calculation which takes into account the mid-point between the highest high and the lowest low over the 52 previous periods, projecting the result 26 periods into the future. Calculating the SSB is therefore similar to the Tenkan and Kijun, just projected ahead of current prices.

- In order to fully understand this line, one can simply look at a weekly chart: the mid-point over the past 52 weeks (one calendar year) is projected 26 weeks (six months) into the future. Such a line appears quite often as a long, flat line on weekly charts given that prices must hit fresh highs or new lows in order to impact the mid-point and bend the line. As a result, **traders should watch closely this price level** on Ichimoku charts as it will often act as a very strong support or resistance.

Chart 1.8: Senkou Span B (SSB)

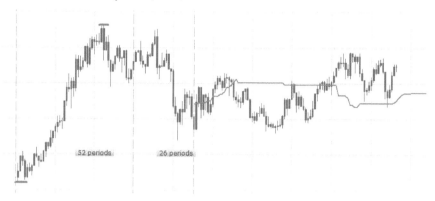

- The **cloud** is the area created between the SSA and the SSB. If the SSA is above the SSB, the cloud is considered bullish. If the SSB is above the SSA however, the cloud is bearish. This reasoning is similar to that of a short moving average being above or below a long moving average.

- The **thickness of the cloud** is determined by the SSA. Given that this line is derived from the average between the Tenkan and the Kijun, the SSA's slope will be in unison with that of the Tenkan and the Kijun during periods where prices move in a strong trend, just in between.

Meanwhile the SSB, which is much less reactive due to the length of its duration input, will remain flat. The distance, or spread, between these two lines will thus lengthen, amplifying the cloud's thickness. **The SSA therefore illustrates past price volatility.**

Likewise, when price movement slows and volatility drops, the SSA will change course and will come back towards the SSB. Crossover of these two lines – known as the **twist** – signals trend reversals as the positioning of the two lines flips.

Chart 1.9: Cloud with labels

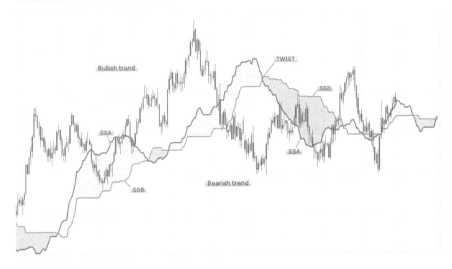

The cloud is hence the heart and soul of Ichimoku as it is the most visible component and offers an understanding of general market conditions and of the trend all at first glance.

The unique aspect of this indicator allows traders to have a deep, multi-temporal understanding of supports and resistances that represent the workings and dynamics of the market studied.

The cloud exemplifies the notion of equilibrium, Ichimoku's unique feature, in a masterful way. **When inside it, the market is considered to be non-directional with a high degree of uncertainty.** Prices that were beforehand considered to be in an uptrend or downtrend (above or beneath the cloud) and that attempt to cross the cloud tell traders that the trend is evolving and that the market is trying to change direction. The way in which prices emerge from the cloud provides information on the direction that the market has chosen, whether it be the former trend or a new one. **The cloud's thickness is therefore critical insofar as it will be easier for prices to cross a twist rather than a large mass.** The concept of support/resistance is clearly visible in the sense that the cloud's shape indicates the probability of a trend reversal in the future.

Chikou Span (Lagging Span – LS)

The Lagging Span is Ichimoku's second distinctive feature: it represents the **current closing prices plotted 26 periods backwards**. Since only closing prices are involved, candlestick shadows (D-D') are not accounted for. In the rest of this book, the term Lagging Span will be used instead of Chikou Span in order to avoid confusion with the Senkou Span lines making up the cloud. Usage of this term will also allow for a better appreciation of the fact that this component 'lags' behind current prices.

Chart 1.10: Chikou Span (Lagging Span)

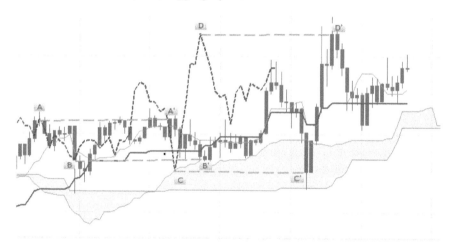

The Lagging Span's precision is striking (C-C'): prices come in contact with the bottom of the cloud while the Lagging Span does the same thing just above the SSA. So it can explain why prices stopped falling in the middle of nowhere.

Finally, segments (A-A') and (B-B') show how the Lagging Span interacts with prices: it halts at the exact level of the Doji's body at point (A) and similarly at the closing price of the red candlestick at point B. Note that at point (B'), current price is testing the support provided by the SSA.

This line can be interpreted as the **market's memory** insofar as it allows the situation of current market prices to be compared with those 26 periods in the past. This underlines price levels that were important in the past and that traders might have forgotten or just ignored due to the lack of knowledge of the asset studied.

While the cloud indicates future levels of support and resistance as well as a zone of equilibrium, the Lagging Span **hints to potential price movements in the making** by reminding traders of important levels tested by the market in the past.

The **cyclical behaviour of prices** is another key concept taught here: prices constantly return to significant support/resistance levels in the market, a little bit like a ball in a pinball game.

The Lagging Span reminds traders of former obstacles by portraying current prices in the past. It will react in the same way as prices do when the market comes into contact with the Kijun or the cloud, for example. Crossovers of the Kijun or the SSB by the Lagging Span further validate initial movements in current prices, thereby confirming the start of trend reversals and above all the potential of follow-through. **This potential is determined by the absence of obstacles or freedom of movement that the Lagging Span faces.**

The Lagging Span can be considered as the **key to unlocking the secret** of validating price movements with Ichimoku, making it a vital element in any trading strategy.

Temporal active space of Ichimoku

The strength of the different lines of this indicator is not only to be found in the simplicity of their calculation of mid-points but rather in describing variations of prices in an extended temporal space.

The chart below explains how the different information overlaps on a certain time interval.

Chart 1.11: Ichimoku's temporal space

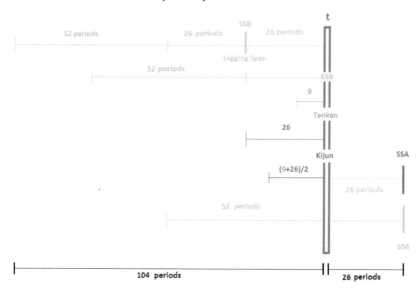

The red vertical line indicates the actual market price and the five lines of the indicator are described according to the length of time in their calculation. A great amount of information appears through the 104 periods prior to the present time (red line). If an asset is observed on a weekly basis, 104 periods represents 2 × 52 weeks, that is two years of prices.

For example, when a Lagging Span encounters an SSB line at the present time, it means that the actual price is set regarding a mid-point of the 52 + 26 periods before, i.e. one year and a half. In the same way, prices which encounter an SSB line at the present time are in fact facing the mid-point of the past year and a half. And, in 26 periods ahead (six months), the market will face the mid-point established today from the year before.

The same reasoning is applied whatever the time frame and this is the fundamental aspect of Ichimoku: the overlap of time through their calculation and their position in the system.

The equilibrium embodied by the mid-points on a large time spectrum is really the secret key of this indicator.

In summary

Ichimoku is made up of:

- Two lines representing mid-points over 9 and 26 periods, the Tenkan Sen and the Kijun Sen, which are interpreted in the same manner as with moving averages. Particular attention is given to the Kijun as it is the signal line. Together, these two lines show **market balance in the present**.

- A cloud setting out a zone of price equilibrium over the last 17 and 52 periods that is projected 26 periods forward and indicates upcoming supports/resistances. In other terms, **the cloud is current market balance shifted into the future**.

- A line not calculated that illustrates current closing prices plotted in the past, thereby embodying the **market's memory**.

Ichimoku is an integral system for market analysis because it stretches over an extended time horizon: current prices are compared in the past via the Lagging Span, and the cloud projects both the past and the present into the future.

Chart 1.12: Ichimoku's construction

The interaction between the lines and prices is the expression of situations of equilibrium and disequilibrium in the market, which, through the observation of key movements, allows traders to understand and to anticipate future investment opportunities.

To arrive at this stage, it's necessary to fully understand the value of each individual element in Ichimoku in order to decipher useful information in interpreting markets. This is the subject discussed in the next chapter.

2

READING ICHIMOKU CHARTS

Ichimoku is a **unique system for understanding markets**: it works self-sufficiently by providing all the elements that are necessary and effective for planning investment strategies.

Interpreting all the five lines that make up this indicator is done simultaneously. With each line's calculation depending on different time horizons, the various output values contribute to the establishment of a set of information that must be understood in its entirety in order to make decisions in the markets. This is explained in more detail below.

The cloud (area between the SSA and the SSB)

The cloud is the main innovation in Ichimoku. It can be seen as a kind of road map that allows traders to immediately recognise the trend and its momentum as well as to easily identify levels of support/resistance that may halt prices, both in the present and within the next 26 periods.

Chart 2.1: Interaction between prices and the cloud

Chart 2.1 illustrates the interaction between prices and the cloud. At the beginning of the chart, prices attempt to cross the cloud but fall back inside it until reaching point (a), thus failing to validate the trend change. This reversal is only effective once prices rise above the cloud later on.

Another hesitant attempt of a trend reversal is evident at point (b) where prices once again fail to break the bottom of the cloud. Prices are pushed back towards the top of the cloud, which offers resistance at point (c) and causes prices to fall back to the bottom of the cloud at which time they break it, thus validating the formation of a bearish trend.

Prices continue following this downtrend while remaining below the cloud until point (d) where they attempt again to mark a new trend but are blocked by the cloud's SSA. After a while, prices succeed in crossing up to the top of the cloud before falling back to the bottom, which serves as support and keeps the market from falling back into a bearish trend.

Finally, one should take note of the capacity of prices to follow the cloud's edge like at point (f). The twist below is an alert for traders as prices could easily break this weak support in order to validate the downtrend that was blocked at point (e).

In a well-defined trend, the cloud gives information on the direction and strength of the trend on top of supports and resistances that prices will likely come across all along this movement.

Chart 2.2: Cloud resistance

Here, the trend is clearly bearish and well represented by the pink cloud that follows prices lower and acts as strong resistance each time prices try to break through it. It thus preserves the direction of price action.

Starting at point (A) where prices pierce the bottom of the cloud, thus validating the transition from an uptrend to a downtrend, the Tenkan and the Kijun follow prices lower. When the market rebounds and breaks these two lines to the upside, the cloud serves as the last resistance (circles). Only at point (B) do prices reach the end of this bearish trend and cross a weak, flat part of the cloud from the bottom up.

Finally, the last interpretation of the cloud will focus on the future as it constitutes a projection of past equilibrium in a time horizon of 26 periods. This singular construction gives traders confirmation of a trend reversal.

Chart 2.3: Future twist

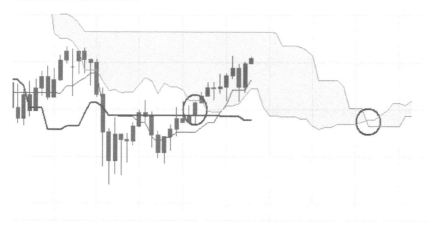

On the far right of chart 2.3, one can see a cloud 'twist' that appears when the SSA crosses the SSB. Here, the cross is bullish as the short-term line cuts across the long-term line to the upside. On top of that, the inflection occurs at the same time as prices break through the Kijun. The information provided by the market tells traders that prices, which were in a range below the Kijun, are likely to cross the cloud in order to validate the trend change. The blue cloud that appears confirms the bullish price action and starts to rise.

The information here relies solely on the future because, technically, current prices find themselves within the cloud and are thereby considered in a state of equilibrium as well as in a zone mired by uncertainty. The market lacks a clear trend in principle.

However, the cloud in itself as no predictive value. It only represents the outcome of the current price movement. As the SSB is slower to move due to the length of its duration input and the SSA is faster in its representation of price movement, a change in the direction of the trend produces a cross of these two lines. It's a simple mathematical effect. One doesn't need to notice this twist at the present time to establish the direction of the market. The breakout of the Kijun logically entails a bullish move of prices.

To end with the cloud twist, when prices arrive at this level there is a potential danger of passing through and breaking with the previous trend. This is by rights a zone to keep a close eye on.

Chart 2.4: Twist and potential trend change

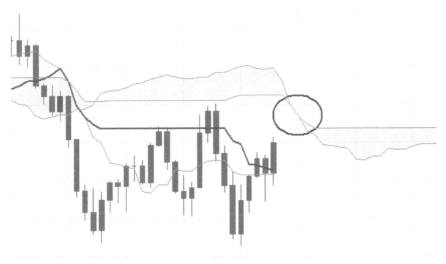

In chart 2.4, if prices continue rising as they have recently been doing, they may very well cross through the cloud twist and validate a bullish trend. One sees, however, that prices have already attempted a trend reversal before but were blocked by the cloud resistance. As the twist is a 'lack of cloud', a second test should be successful.

Chart 2.5: Twist and cloud break by prices

Here are two examples of prices passing through cloud twists:

At point (A), prices break through to the downside, then the pink cloud acts as resistance, validating the trend reversal.

At point (C), there is a superb piercing of the twist by prices whereas they had previously failed at point (B). Sometimes, a bit of patience is needed in order to validate a trend reversal as prices tend often to want to follow a path of least resistance.

Through these multiple interpretations, the cloud is a goldmine of indications in itself. So it is accordingly **the element upon which traders should concentrate their attention** when first looking at a price chart. **The cloud is the centrepiece of this trading system**: the fact that it spreads over a wide time horizon gives it a high importance that will be reinforced through interpretation of the other lines.

The Tenkan Sen (nine periods)

Being the weakest line in Ichimoku, **the Tenkan primarily indicates the strength of the short-term trend through the degree of its slope**. And as it follows price movements closely, it serves as an immediate support/resistance that, if broken, signals an alert on the longevity of the current trend.

Chart 2.6: Tenkan Sen

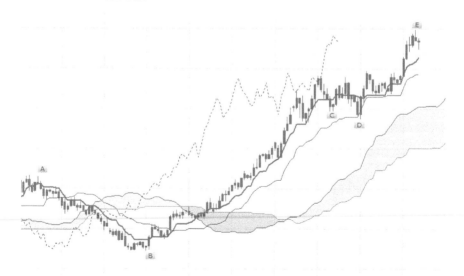

Chart 2.6 above shows how the Tenkan (red line) follows prices when they are in a clear trend (A–B). A break in the opposite direction takes place at point (B), alerting traders that the downtrend may be finished. A couple of candlesticks later, prices test the Tenkan and confirm the change in the market's trend. Prices find themselves once again in tandem with this line which has a strong slope (B–C). A new alert appears at point (C): they consolidate around the Tenkan, indicating uncertainty in which direction the market will move in the future. A new break at point (D) revitalises the bullish trend up until point (E), where prices seem to want to consolidate. The Tenkan has a strong slope though, allowing traders to anticipate renewed buying pressure later on.

The Kijun Sen (26 periods)

The Kijun is **one of the most important lines in Ichimoku**. Given that it takes into account a larger number of periods in calculating price mid-points, long plateaus take shape when prices are not trending (no higher highs or lower lows). The notion of balance comes to light via extremely **reliable levels of support/resistance** making up the basic information provided by the Kijun.

Chart 2.7: Kijun Sen

Indeed, the Kijun is the second obstacle that prices face once they have broken through the Tenkan. So, if prices bounce off the Kijun, the break in the trend is merely a brief breather, or pullback, in the market before it resumes. On the other hand, if prices pass through the Kijun, the direction of the prevailing movement becomes obsolete. A new trend takes shape so long as the technical break is not invalidated by prices returning to the other side of the Kijun.

Reading price charts allows traders to immediately identify the positioning of prices with respect to this line. If they are too far from it, they will likely come back to it because the Kijun is a point of equilibrium in the market. The notion of mean reversion comes into play here: taking a look at the Fibonacci levels on chart 2.8, one can see that the Kijun corresponds exactly with 50% of the movement that was retraced by the market.

Chart 2.8: Kijun and Fibonacci retracement

Traders should also take great value of price behaviour when the market comes into contact with the Kijun. Prices will either bounce off the Kijun or they will break it, thereby making two different signals traders should watch for.

It is therefore important to locate prices with respect to this line so as to judge **possible obstacles** during the lifetime of a given trend. **Any time prices encounter a Kijun, it will be a strong obstacle to be dealt with.** This is a price zone that will likely be worked on a bit by the market given that the Kijun represents price equilibrium.

The Lagging Span

In addition to the cloud, the Lagging Span is **the second innovation in Ichimoku**. As mentioned in Chapter 1, the term 'Lagging Span' is preferred to its Japanese name (Chikou Span) because it helps to avoid confusion with the Senkou Span lines making up the cloud and better captures the fact that this line lags behind current prices.

By sending current prices into the past, it represents the market's memory.

Chart 2.9: Lagging Span

Without the need of any calculation, this simple line representing **current closing prices** will act just like them when facing the various obstacles ahead of it.

The main difference between current market prices and the Lagging Span is that the latter confronts **previous** levels of support/resistance.

For example, at point (A) the Lagging Span was blocked by the bottom of the cloud. In order to fully understand what happened, it is necessary to imagine the candlestick's shadow, which does not directly appear since the line only considers closing prices. It filters the internal noises of the considered period by the candlestick. While current prices seem to halt in the middle of nowhere, their bounce can be explained by the Lagging Span.

Ichimoku requires fully grasping this dual interpretation of prices. The example presented above (chart 2.9) is of the German DAX index viewed in a monthly time frame. Point (A) represents the end of the stock market crash in March 2009. Interestingly, it was the only stock index to give such information. Investors who knew how to correctly interpret this indicator at the time understood that the fall in the markets had reached its end and that they could start buying stocks again.

At point (B), the Lagging Span is blocked by the top of the candlestick even if prices fell much further during the month as the current red candlestick's shadow shows. Thus, a double support has acted in the market: that of the Lagging Span and that of current prices.

At point (C), the Lagging Span meets resistance at the cloud's SSA, causing current market prices to fall even though they seem to be in the middle of nowhere. The market falls back to the Kijun, which corresponds with the Lagging Span coming into contact with the shadow of a candlestick.

Finally, in the same manner as we saw with current prices, the Lagging Span can also pass through cloud twists (on the far left of the chart).

Chart 2.10 below illustrates a classic case where prices are in a bearish trend below the cloud, but the Lagging Span influences the direction of the market by crossing the cloud twist and entering a more bullish trend. This dichotomy between the mirror image of prices and prices themselves triggers a period of hesitation during which the Lagging Span bounces several times off the cloud's SSA (support) and prices interact with the Tenkan (resistance).

Chart 2.10: Lagging Span and prices

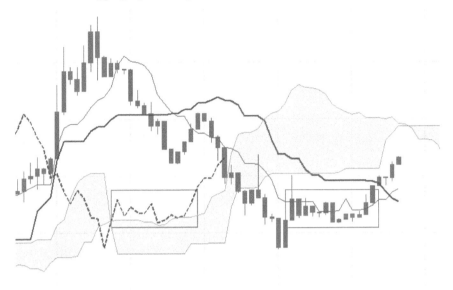

The upward movement in prices, which should allow the market to eventually rise above the cloud and thus enter a bullish trend, only takes shape once the Kijun gives in to buying pressure.

These examples show the imperative need for traders to analyse both representations of prices together, as one reinforces the interpretation of the other. This simultaneous analysis is used to explain price action already underway, and anticipate interruptions in trends or the beginning of new ones.

In this system of market analysis, **the Lagging Span is there to help decipher price behaviour and to evaluate the potential of a movement. It is an unavoidable element in any analysis and entry or exit setup in the markets.** As we will see later on, it is essential in trading when monitoring an open position.

Now, how can the trader combine all the various information provided by the components of Ichimoku in order to obtain the best understanding of the market studied and to formulate an investment strategy?

This is what we are going to explore in the next chapter.

3

ANALYSIS

Having examined the various components that make up Ichimoku and how to interpret them, we will now focus on how to analyse charts using only this indicator.

This chapter will also introduce another concept in the temporal scope of Ichimoku: analysis of markets in different time frames. In the first two chapters of this book, we focused on the fact that Ichimoku provided a glance of the markets over an extended time horizon. In what follows here, we will see that **in order to fully understand the way markets are moving, it is necessary – even critical – to study them on different time frames**.

While the first two chapters relied primarily on a purely technical description of Ichimoku, this chapter and the next will adopt a more personalised approach as analytical styles vary from analyst to analyst. But the fundamental principles of interpretation, such as those created by Goichi Hosoda, are entirely respected.

This system of market reading is exactly the one applied by Japanese professional traders I happened to recently work with. I was thus able to confirm and validate my trading method with Ichimoku.

Three examples using different time frames (TF)

Example 1: GBPUSD (pound sterling/US dollar)

Chart 3.1: Monthly chart of the GBPUSD

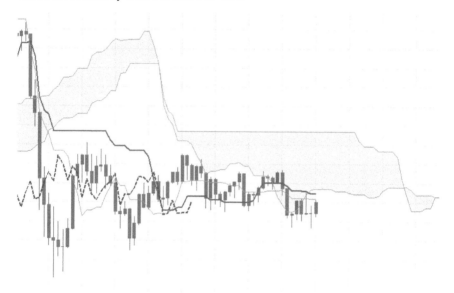

When one is unfamiliar with a market and wants to study it in depth, it is a good idea to start with a **monthly chart**.

The first reflex of the trader should be to take note of where prices are in relation to the cloud. In this case, they are below a relatively thick and horizontal cloud, which indicates the lack of a clear trend in the market. Looking at recent price action, this is exactly the case.

Looking forward, I'm hardly interested in the projected cloud that has turned blue, hinting to a bullish change in direction whereas prices remain range-bound. Only the form of the cloud in the future and possible areas of weakness catch my attention. In this case, the cloud's thickness remains constant, and the twist is quite distant.

Taking only the cloud into account, my opinion is neutral or even bearish on this currency pair.

Looking at Ichimoku's lines, two elements confirm this assessment. The first is that of the double resistance formed by the Tenkan and the Kijun that prices are testing. They must rise above these lines in order for a bullish movement to really take shape in the market. I put forward a bullish hypothesis on the grounds that prices don't seem to want to fall further even though they are under the cloud. They are range-bound.

The second element is that of the Lagging Span that will or will not confirm the possibility or potential for prices to rise. This line is struggling to emerge from under the Kijun and seems to want to test it again. The bullish potential is rightly determined by the break of the Kijun by the Lagging Span on the same level as the Tenkan for the current prices. But the target is not worth pursuing, with the Kijun and the SSA just above. These two lines should act as strong resistance.

My conclusion for this time frame is that prices are capped by a double resistance and that the bullish potential indicated by the Lagging Span is limited. On top of that, the thickness of the cloud is an obstacle for a true British pound rally. Given this, my opinion on this market is bearish.

So as to refine this analysis, I will now zoom in on a smaller time frame: **the weekly chart**.

Chart 3.2: Weekly chart of the GBPUSD

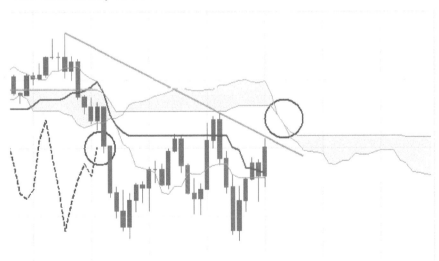

The same procedures to analyse the market are reproduced here:

- Prices are below the cloud but are nearing a twist, which may indicate an upcoming trend reversal if the market breaks through the cloud.

- Prices are supported by both the Tenkan and the Kijun. So long as this double support holds, I'll remain bullish. On the other hand, prices are testing a triple resistance composed of a trend line (this is the only additional information I add to charts as it is useful in trading) and the Kijun in line with the SSB line of the cloud. Take good note of this setup because the convergence of these two lines on the same level always represents strong support/resistance. Indeed, it is important to remember their construction as the Kijun, taking into account 26 periods, is a reliable line of strong support/resistance while the SSB is based on 52 periods (2 × 26) and projection ahead of current prices. The SSB is the most robust part of the cloud and of Ichimoku altogether. Therefore, when both lines are at the same price level, they offer strong support/resistance that should not be ignored. In such a situation, my first bullish impression ends up a bit mixed.

- Finally, looking at the Lagging Span helps to adjust the bullish argument in the sense that it is facing past prices represented by large candlesticks. Breaking through this area will not be an easy task. Furthermore, supposing that the Lagging Span does overcome this obstacle, other resistances are close by with the Tenkan and the Kijun side-by-side as well as the SSB above.

To conclude on this time frame, bullish potential is weak but no bearish signal will be given so long as prices remain above their support. My final opinion is therefore neutral.

Now I will zoom in on an even smaller time frame with the **daily chart**.

Chart 3.3: Daily chart of the GBPUSD

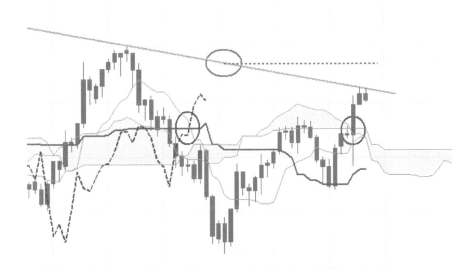

My first impression is much different from the other two time frames: prices are **above** the cloud and are not facing any immediate resistance as the Lagging Span is likewise free to rise further.

One can thus see a trend reversal with prices having crossed the cloud twist. In this time frame, the trend is now clearly bullish.

However, there still remains one obstacle to overcome: the bearish trend line that is already hampering the market's rally and this will be tested by the Lagging Span after current prices will have broken resistance. The upward price target will be initially limited to this level shown by the red dotted line.

To sum up, I have analysed the Cable with three different time frames: bearish on the monthly chart, neutral on the weekly chart and bullish on the daily chart. One might legitimately think that there is an inconsistency here and that the interpretation of this currency pair using Ichimoku has led to contradictory conclusions, making it inapt as a decision-making tool. In fact, as disturbing as it may seem, there is not any contradiction.

If I go back to the very beginning with the bullish information from the daily chart, I realise that it corresponds with the blue candlestick as well as the Lagging Span that is currently rising on the monthly chart. You may have already noticed that when I first analysed the market in this time frame, I interpreted the different elements on the chart with a purely bullish perspective.

I did not mention the bearish potential beyond the fact that prices were below the cloud and therefore *de facto* in a downtrend.

Likewise, on the weekly chart, I only highlighted the possible obstacles to the bullish price movement. Again, I did not comment on the probability of prices falling back into a downtrend.

Lastly, the trend being clearly bullish on the daily chart, there was no bearish potential to even mention.

It turns out then that despite all the bearish indicators in the beginning, the whole of my analysis was done with a bullish stance. The reason for this is due to the first glance of the bullish candlestick on the monthly chart, comforted by rising prices above a double support on the weekly chart. In zooming in on smaller time frames, I only dissected the rising monthly candlestick and come to the conclusion that the trend reversal underway on the daily chart will only last for a short period of time if the monthly resistances play their role.

Through this example, one can see that Ichimoku – from its construction and its various lines – covers an extensive time span and indicates important support/resistance levels for more than just one time frame. It is necessary to look at different time frames together in order to better understand the overall direction of the market studied and its potential. So, the trader should choose three time frames according to their investment time horizon.

Example 2: AUDUSD (Australian dollar/US dollar)

This second example is meant to demonstrate that the same system of analysis and its relevance can be applied to even smaller time frames.

The day trader looking for short-term opportunities will usually start with the **240-minute** chart to get an overall idea of price action.

Chart 3.4: 240-minute chart of the AUDUSD

We need to first start with looking at price action, which is bullish as the market is trading above the cloud. Prices seem to want to bounce off the SSB with a Doji candlestick currently taking shape. One should note, however, the cloud twist further ahead that will need to be watched closely if prices end up consolidating laterally over the next several days. After prices, the next thing to note is the Lagging Span which, after having validated the current trend by crossing the cloud twist, has fallen back within the thin cloud. By dipping back into the cloud without being able to truly break free from it, the Lagging Span indicates certain indecision in this new trend, evident in recent price action.

It then seems necessary to consider shorter time frames in order to understand this currency pair's price action and above all what one could expect going forward.

Chart 3.5: 60-minute chart of the AUDUSD

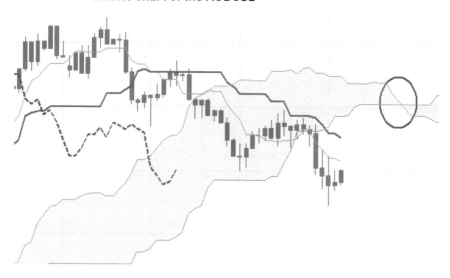

The **60-minute chart** shows a more bearish trend with an attempt by price to rebound as shown by the last two blue candlesticks, which represent the lower shadow of the Doji in the 240-minute chart. The information that may support my bullish bias is the twist further above, provided that the market rises above the Tenkan and the Kijun. The Lagging Span is in a neutral position as it is still inside the cloud, limiting the immediate risk of extended losses.

Note that since the bearish break of the Kijun by the market, prices have tried to invalidate this signal by retesting the Kijun on two different occasions, both without any success.

Chart 3.6: 15-minute chart of the AUDUSD

Now looking at the **15-minute chart**, the trend is clearly bearish with prices rebounding in the direction of the Kijun, which corresponds to the Tenkan on the 60-minute chart. The Kijun is at the same level as the SSB (right-hand side of the chart) giving weight to its importance as a resistance. If prices were to break through the Kijun, they would likely rise towards another resistance at the SSB just above.

At this stage of the analysis, the initial bullish stance loses merit given the major obstacles that prices must overcome in smaller time frames in order to revitalise buying pressure. The fact that the Lagging Span is in a neutral area in the 240-minute chart takes on its full meaning here.

Finally, the **5-minute chart** (chart 3.7) gives a more optimistic view.

Chart 3.7: 5-minute chart of the AUDUSD

The market is approaching a cloud twist but the Lagging Span still must rise above prices and the Kijun in order to confirm the bullish potential. The day trader should wait for prices to cross the cloud to the upside and for the Lagging

Span to break the Kijun: this will validate the possible rise in prices seen on the 240-minute chart with the Doji candlestick and the bounce off the SSB.

The two following charts (5-minutes and 240-minutes, chart 3.8 and chart 3.9 respectively) show the outcome of price actions.

Chart 3.8: 5-minute chart of the AUDUSD

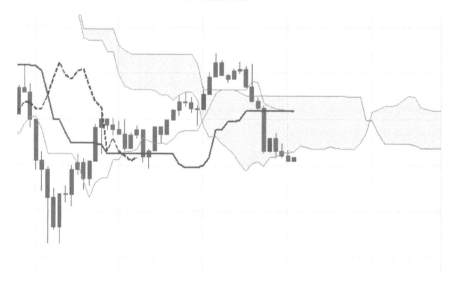

Prices indeed crossed the cloud twist, and the Lagging Span broke the Kijun. The number of buyers in the market having obviously not been large enough, this rally was aborted as prices fell back into the cloud and broke the Kijun, thereby invalidating the buy signal. As for the Lagging Span, it did not even try to rise above the cloud, which in itself was an indication that there was not enough buying pressure behind this price action.

Chart 3.9: 240-minute chart of the AUDUSD

Finally, the Doji candlestick seen before in the 240-minute chart ended up closing in the shape of a bullish hammer, but this signal was not validated by the market immediately after. Prices are now falling back towards the SSB, joined by the Kijun which adds to the strength of the support.

Concerning the Lagging Span, it is still falling within the cloud.

No final decision can be made on this currency pair so long as the support defined by the cloud is intact.

To conclude, using shorter time frames requires waiting for solid validation by all Ichimoku's lines.

In the case just studied, the bullish trend was not validated in the leading time frame (240 minutes) since the Lagging Span was still inside the cloud and falling. The impression that prices could rise needed further proof to confirm the bullish potential.

Here, the need of being able to juggle quickly between different time frames without modifying settings and with a single reading is crucial in order to fully grasp the direction and the potential in the markets easily.

Example 3: USDJPY (US dollar/Japanese yen)

Here's a last example of a market in a strong trend.

Chart 3.10: 60-minute chart of the USDJPY

In this **60-minute chart**, the currency pair is without a doubt in an uptrend with the Tenkan following prices closely. However, this movement has stalled as indicated by the Kijun flattening out while the Tenkan continues its steep rise. We then need to examine smaller time frames to verify if there is a danger of breaking the Tenkan, which would be considered an alert on the longevity of the current trend.

We will take a look at the **15-minute chart**:

Chart 3.11: 15-minute chart of the USDJPY

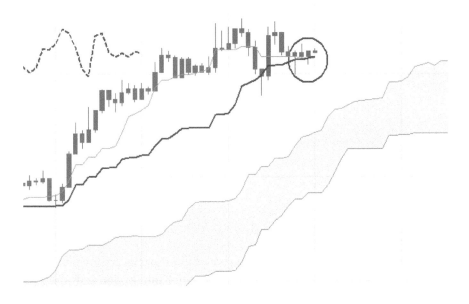

Prices are in fact in a dangerous area since they are testing the double support formed by the Tenkan and the Kijun. A break below this level would imply a correction towards the cloud with the Lagging Span falling below prices. The bullish trend would then be in danger.

Chart 3.12: 5-minute chart of the USDJPY

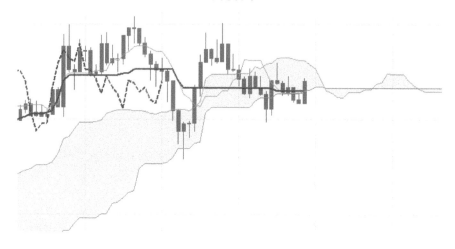

This **5-minute chart** (chart 3.12) does a good job at showing price action on the support identified before that corresponds to the Kijun in line with the SSB. The Lagging Span, despite having broken below the Kijun, does not confirm the bearish potential as it is currently bouncing off the top of the cloud. This is an indication that the bearish potential is minute.

Indeed, the bullish trend resumes shortly after this simple breather in the market.

Chart 3.13: 15-minute chart of the USDJPY

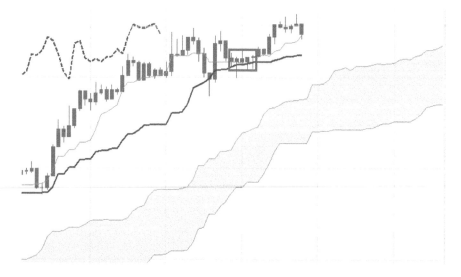

In chart 3.13, an **updated 15-minute chart**, the Kijun acted as support, and prices set off higher in breaking the Tenkan. Take note of the spread between these two lines that appears after prices start to rise, giving the Tenkan once again the role of signalling alerts and the Kijun the role of the final support.

Chart 3.14: 60-minute chart of the USDJPY

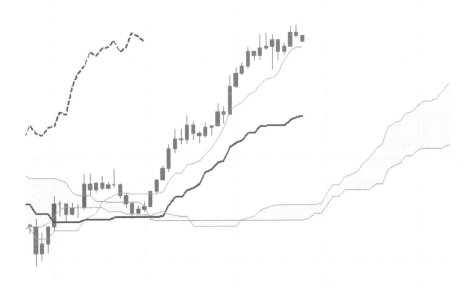

In the **updated 60-minute chart**, chart 3.14, no alert was given as prices never broke below the Tenkan.

Methodology

From the examples just seen, remember the following:

1. The process of analysing the markets is always done in the same way:

- Where are prices located in relation to the cloud and what is the latter's trend?
- How far away are the Tenkan and Kijun, levels of support/resistance, from current prices?
- Where is the Lagging Span, and what immediate obstacles does it face?

Analysis is concentrated on current and past prices, and conclusions are drawn from their position within the system of lines that make up Ichimoku.

2. The next step in the analysis is to evaluate each line's contribution to the overall understanding of the market studied:

- Where are prices with respect to the Tenkan? Are they supported by this line, or are there any alerts given?
- Are prices near a Kijun providing support/resistance, or are they currently passing through this important line?
- Where are prices in relation to the cloud, and above all, what is their distance from one of the two lines that belong to it? The SSA is more easily broken than the SSB. And a twist will be crossed more easily than a thick cloud.
- Does the Lagging Span, the cornerstone of the system, confirm current price action? What obstacles might hinder its movement and thereby block prices?

3. Lastly, this interpretation is then repeated on other time frames chosen by the trader in accordance with the investment strategy's time horizon:

- The highest time frame is used to define the general state of the market.
- One time frame lower allows the trader to refine his initial anticipation in the market and to identify sensitive points.
- A trading strategy can be established on one last, shorter time frame.

Planning a trading strategy, realising it by entering the market and concluding it by closing the position are all subjects that are covered in the next chapter dedicated to trading in the broad sense.

PART 2

ICHIMOKU IN PRACTICE

4

TRADING

Before explaining how to enter trades and to manage them with Ichimoku, I would like to emphasise the difference between analysts and traders. It is necessary to distinguish between the two because, according to the role taken on by readers, the various chart elements will not be looked at in the same way and the way in which verdicts are made will differ.

Analysts v traders

Analysts adopt a neutral position when studying charts. They aim at **describing situations**, at detecting major market movements and at deducing strategic assumptions of what will happen next. They do not get emotionally involved.

In the case of Ichimoku charts, analysts first take a look at the cloud's position in order to get a first impression of the general trend. They then examine where prices stand with respect to the cloud for the purpose of determining if the trend is still valid or changing.

Analysts then study the Lagging Span in order to ascertain whether or not it validates current price action.

Only at the end of this process do analysts look at the Tenkan and the Kijun in order to refine the analysis of the market's position, evaluate its near-term potential and establish a strategy.

For example, in chart 4.1, analysts would consider the trend to be neutral seeing that the cloud is flat. However, prices are below the cloud, meaning that they are likely to keep on falling.

Chart 4.1: Weekly chart of the GBPUSD

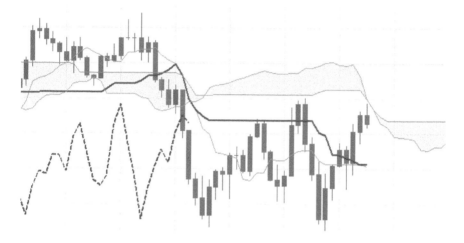

On the other hand, attention should be given to the cloud twist and to how close prices are to this point as a break above would indicate a change in the trend. The probability of such a reversal is reinforced by the fact that a support, formed by the Kijun situated at the same level as the SSB (top of the cloud to the right), is close by. Depending on whether this support holds or not, the assumption of a break higher will or will not be validated.

Finally, the Lagging Span is also bearish but is currently crossing prices, which is the first step to a trend reversal. It still has to rise above the Kijun, but will then face resistance from a previous Kijun to the left that's in line with the bottom of the cloud. The progression of the Lagging Span will be difficult and will weigh on that of prices as they will no longer face any real obstacle to the upside.

From an analyst's point of view, the strategy is therefore the following: in the event of prices crossing the cloud twist, the trend will change from bearish to bullish. The market's upside potential will be confirmed once the Lagging Span will also have risen above the cloud, which will not be an easy task to accomplish.

The invalidation of this strategy, and therefore the confirmation that prices are in a bearish trend, will be effective if the market breaks below the Kijun/SSB support.

Analysts evaluate the possible scenarios of future price action based upon the cloud and the Lagging Span, both of which are the two Ichimoku elements that provide the most salient information. The Kijun is only considered at the end of the analysis because it is located within the cloud's SSB and reinforces these levels; furthermore, it acts as a resistance for the Lagging Span.

As for **traders**, they will adopt a different approach due to the fact that **their goal is to seek opportunities to make profit** in a given market. In addition to analysing the market and retaining the same information previously mentioned, they will convert it into potential market entry strategies. So, traders also focus on the distances between each of the technical levels identified and calculate possible profit or losses based on them.

Furthermore, traders also have to take into consideration a factor that analysts are not concerned with: **emotions or fear** that must be controlled once a position is taken in the market. In their analysis, they look to limit these psychological effects by identifying all the elements that will either confirm or invalidate their strategies. All the Ichimoku components are meticulously examined in order to bring to light the most relevant information. Other technical analysis tools may even be employed to refine certain areas of doubt.

If we reconsider the previous example, here is the additional information that traders must deal with in depth (see chart 4.2):

Chart 4.2: GBPUSD and its trend line

1. Prices did not succeed in breaking through the cloud twist, and the market closed below the SSB/Kijun resistance level. This leads one to think that prices may resume their bearish trend the following week. However, by adding a trend line to the chart, the market close no longer seems as bearish as before because prices stopped falling once this line was reached. A rebound is therefore possible, and the assumption that the market will pass through the cloud twist should not be disregarded.

2. As for the Lagging Span, traders notice the cloud twist that lies ahead if it succeeds in breaking the double resistance composed of the SSB and the Kijun. This information is also critical because it demonstrates the strength of this resistance and indicates that a definitive break above would be an even more reliable signal.

The strategy developed by traders is more detailed than the one considered by analysts. In this example, traders add the following details to the strategy: so long as the market is trading above the trend line, the possibility of a cloud break remains valid. The Lagging Span should be watched closely for such a resistance break in addition to its behaviour as it rises towards the SSB and crosses through the cloud twist.

On the other hand, a break below this trend line will invalidate the bullish scenario and will confirm the current bearish potential with a target at the Tenkan/Kijun cluster.

So, the trading plan conceived here will give a precise entry point, an invalidation level (or stop-loss) and an exit point. In fact, **traders know exactly their expected profit and the amount of their potential losses in accordance with their money management**. Once the position has been taken, the risk will have already been evaluated, and all the levels likely to pose obstacles to price action will have already been identified as potential entry/exit points. The trade is under control and stress is minimised.

To sum up, **the main difference between analysts and traders** is the emotional commitment faced by the latter whereas the former remains neutral and indifferent throughout the process of analysing the market. Even if the overall vision of the market is the same, the resulting interpretation will not have the same degree of precision. And let us not forget that traders must first be good analysts, while pure analysts are hardly ever traders.

To practise these two activities on a daily basis, the way in which I study charts is not at all the same. The underlying analysis is of course the same, but when I look at charts as a trader I scan all of Ichimoku's lines, respecting each one's importance with regard to the information provided. Even though this indicator alone is sufficient in 95% of cases, I sometimes add other tools such as trend lines, especially for very short-term trades. Like in the example above, this allows me to avoid invalidating strategies too early and to hold on to positions that seem to contradict my analysis.

In addition to this simple analysis based only on Ichimoku principles, there is another system of reading a chart as important as the one described above and which has to be taken into consideration by traders. I name it: Dynamic Market Reading.

Dynamic Market Reading

Whatever the asset chosen, an index, a share, a currency pair or a commodity, the market is the place of exchange between buyers and sellers. The interaction of these two opposing parties is represented by the price, the net result of the supply and the demand of the asset.

The variation of prices is the consequence of the adjustment between supply and demand at a given moment, that is to say a break in equilibrium between buyers and sellers. The life of the market is thus made up of increases, decreases or stagnation, depending on the activity of the actors.

The charts that are used to analyse an asset visually represent these price changes. We thus visualise a sequence of prices over time.

If we want a global view of the price evolution of an asset, we can look at a simple line. The information that will be obtained will be elementary and difficult to exploit in trading.

The best way of representing prices for both analysis and trading is using Japanese candlesticks. Each candlestick represents for a given time frame, the opening and closing prices (body) and the high and low reached during the period (shadow). They give us a good reading of the interactions between the market players, both from a static point of view of analysis and in a dynamic way when it comes to trading (i.e. for position management).

I will not explain here all the various candlestick patterns, this can be found in many other books. But I will explain how to analyse them and use them in trading.

A price, or more exactly its change over a given period of time, is the result of the exchanges that take place between market players. It is therefore a quantified representation of human behaviour by translating the actions and feelings of the participants.

The Japanese candlestick allows us to better understand the emotional state of the market and to quickly grasp its changes in sentiment over time.

When we read a candlestick the first thing we look at is its colour: a blue body represents buyers and a red body is for sellers. NB. The choice of colours can usually be configured by the user.

Then we look at the size of the body. The bigger it is, the more buyers and sellers are present with one side driving the market. A small body is a sign of agreement on the price between the two camps, with neither side really having control of the direction of the market. It is a state of equilibrium which is found in the spinning tops or Dojis, the latter having a non-existent body.

Finally, we look at the shadow (also called wick). In my opinion this is essential in the dynamic analysis of price movement. The shadow represents prices hit by the market where players have traded but which are outside the consensus of equilibrium.

What follows is the analysis of some of the major candlestick shapes (from the point of view of a buyer).

Diagram 4.1: Major candlestick shapes

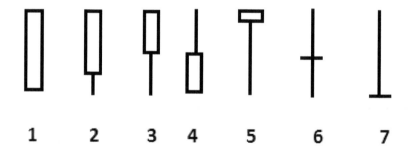

1) A large candlestick that has no shadow (Marubozu) indicates that buyers dominate the market. The trend is strongly upward.

2) The appearance of a shadow indicates that the opposing side shows itself but without taking control. It is often the result of profit taking by the dominant side.

3) A candlestick opening followed by a movement contrary to the direction of the candlestick (colour of the body) can also correspond to profit taking by

buyers. Then the price resumes in the direction of the candlestick with new buyers who enter the market. This creates a shadow and a close on the high point. The dominant camp retains control of the market.

4) A candlestick opening without a shadow indicates the strong presence of buyers. The upper shadow tells us that either the dominant camp succeeded in pushing prices to extremes and then took its gains, or that the opposing camp considers that the price level reached became interesting to enter the market. With this type of configuration, the size of the shadow relative to the body gives the final feeling about the battle between the two camps.

If the size of the shadow is larger than that of the body, it may be that the dominant camp at the opening has closed a large part of its positions, leaving the opposing camp to enter the market and take control.

In an established trend, this can be a warning about a possible change in the psychology of the market.

5) and 6) are the extreme cases called Doji, and the most significant candlestick to give signals of a reversal of a trend.

A very fine or even non-existent body in the central part of the candlestick demonstrates a battle between the two camps. And the longer the shadows, the fiercer the battle. The actors seek extreme prices in both directions but with a return to equilibrium in the end.

Depending on where this type of candlestick appears in the trend, it could be a sign of reversing or simple market hesitation. Any interpretation of the candlestick should be read in context. This type of candlestick appearing on extreme levels after a long trend indicates reversal, whereas if it appears while the trend is in progress it can signal merely a pause.

7) The more specific Dojis whose very fine bodies are at the top or bottom point will have a strong meaning signalling a change in trend. The dragonfly (at a low point of the market) indicates buyers have taken control. And the tombstone (at a high market point) indicates that it is the sellers who become dominant.

In summary, observing a single candlestick in the general context of a trend gives essential information about the current psychology of market players (dominant buyer sentiment or seller). And this can give an indication as to where the market is going next. This is what can give the trader the famous 'feeling' for the market.

The abundant literature on the analysis of Japanese candlesticks includes a form of analysis that I will call *static*; it is a style more appropriate to the cold technical analysis of the market. This incorporates many configurations, such as black clouds, engulfing pattern, soldiers, mountains and ravens. I do not intend to cover these here. Partly because other authors have already done so very well, but also I have a different approach.

In my experience, as a technical analyst and as a trader, I have often found that these configurations have a variable rate of success depending on the chosen time frame. For example, an engulfing pattern is more likely to work on a long time frame (e.g. weekly or daily), than on short or even very short time frames (e.g. one or five minutes).

There will overall be more failures than successes of analysis at short time frames because of market noise. Whereas with longer time frames the absorption of new information by the market is done inside the candlestick. And, thus, a configuration of two or three candlesticks is more representative of the true sentiment of the market.

The main rule in reading candlesticks is to wait for confirmation of the information they give us by a third candlestick. As a side note, we might observe that in Japanese culture the number 3 has special significance in the same way as 8 for the Chinese, or 13 in the West. The 3 is indeed the mark of a start, or reversal, in a series of events. Thus, we find the 3 crows, 3 mountains or the 3 soldiers.

In the West, it is easy to draw a parallel with the waves of Ralph Nelson Elliott. As you are probably aware, in Elliott Wave Theory, price movements are counted in 5 impulsive waves and 3 corrective waves. However, impulsive waves comprise 3 waves in the direction of the main trend (1-3-5) and 2 corrective waves (2-4). We find the 3 impulsive candlesticks. And just as an Elliott Wave follower would position himself preferably on wave 3 (the heart of the trend), the trader will prefer to take the second candlestick, the first giving the signal and the third being able to reject it.

When looking at Japanese candlestick charts this phenomenon is very apparent and very useful to master, especially on short time frames. But the analysis is not as simple as counting 1-2-3. A certain subjectivity is necessary and a good understanding of the formation of candlesticks is important.

On the following chart I have highlighted a few configurations. Some might say that there are many other times when we observe more than three candlesticks of the same colour. This is where dynamic analysis takes its meaning.

Chart 4.3: EURAUD

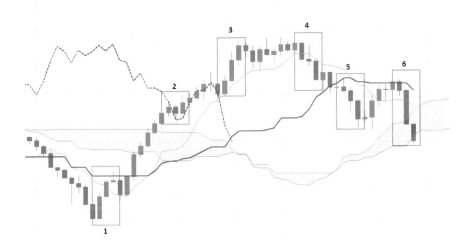

In this example, three blue candlesticks (1) are formed after a bearish movement. This is a correction that goes back to the Kijun, a classic case. The following red candlestick is ignored: it is a test of the Tenkan which is validated and confirms a reversal of upward trend after the Kijun breakout. This impulse takes place with twice three blue candlesticks then we have a consolidation in three candlesticks (2).

The rectangle (3) is a new impulse of three blue candlesticks followed by a consolidation and a correction of three red candlesticks (4). Three candlesticks are needed to break the Kijun which gives a bearish impulse of three red candlesticks (5). A return on the Kijun to validate this fall is done with three blue candlesticks (the Dojis are to be ignored). Finally, the test of the Kijun validates a bearish recovery and the acceleration is done on three red candlesticks (6).

I introduced here the notion of a dynamic reading for trading. A sell signal is given by the break of the Kijun by a small Doji (5). A sell trade is initiated on the first red candlestick whose shadow tested the Kijun and validated. We know that we will stay in the position for three red candlesticks because it is a bearish pulse following a break. The position is unwound as soon as the shadow is formed on the third red candlestick. At this moment an aggressive trader goes long in order to play the correction: he enters the candlestick following the Doji above his high point, being careful that the bearish movement does not continue. And the position remains long for three blue candlesticks. The red Doji is ignored and the exit is done on the third blue candlestick on the Kijun.

The following red candlestick does not confirm the rise, and so a short position is resumed on the second red candlestick and again with a three-candlestick outlook. As soon as the price reaches the bottom of the cloud and the Lagging Span touches the Kijun (6), the trader exits because he knows that a blue correction candlestick will follow. The Lagging Span must bounce before breaking the Kijun and we are on a cloud bottom.

And here is what happens.

Chart 4.4: EURAUD

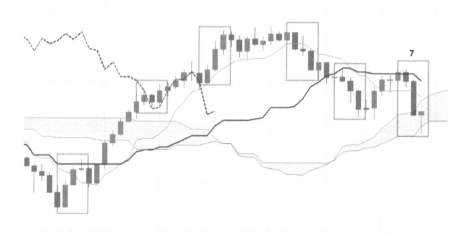

The third red candlestick turns into a blue candlestick (7) with a rebound in price on the bottom of the cloud and the Lagging Span goes up over its Kijun. The exit was opportune.

On the other hand, we do not play the correction here because the resistance formed by the top of the cloud and the Tenkan are too close and do not give enough hope of gains. We wait for the three blue correction candlesticks to be made and validate this resistance before resuming the decline.

Only an aggressive short-term trader looking for a few points would enter the low point of the third red candlestick as he waits for a blue candlestick afterwards. He knows that he enters on a shadow with the objective the Tenkan, a level on which he would exit his position.

Sometimes it happens that one plays a quick counter trend on two shadows: the first (as in this case) and the second shadow signalling the continuation of the price rise to go to a level before turning down and finishing red. Afterwards, we realise that we were buying on a bearish candlestick! It is by switching to shorter time frames that we will notice that these two shadows represent a corrective movement in three candlesticks (see the example of the green circle in chart 4.7).

Chart 4.5: EURAUD

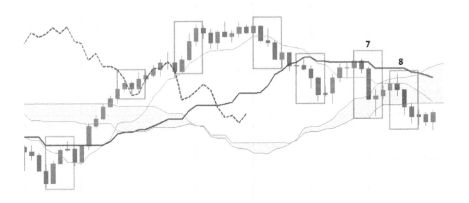

The price movement continues with three red candlesticks (8). Then a consolidation occurs and results in alternating colour candlesticks with non-significant bodies. A new position will only be initiated when the Lagging Span has broken its low cloud.

In trends it is sometimes difficult to see a clear count and it is therefore necessary to use some interpretation. For example, if a first candlestick breaks a Kijun, the count only begins from the second candlestick that becomes the first of the three. This then gives four candlesticks for this impulse.

The appearance of Dojis or spinning tops is often ignored because they are candlesticks of indecision or pause and are therefore not representative of any prevailing impulsive movement.

Chart 4.6: GBPJPY

In chart 4.6, we have some good examples of three-candlestick structures (A-B-D-E) which are perfectly legible.

Box C presents the case where the Dojis are ignored to confirm the count. However, the second Doji dragonfly is also a blue candlestick as buyers have invalidated the decline. Only the next candlestick that closes lower than this Doji confirms the previous drop and gives the third red.

Box F has at first sight four red candlesticks, except the first is not considered because it stops at half of the previous blue candlestick, it is therefore not bearish. We will count only from the following candlestick to get three red.

Box G is a consolidation. In these cases we often find an alternation of colours with bodies being close to equal. The big red candlestick shows us nevertheless that the sellers are always present.

Finally, the large black frame is more difficult and uses a slightly different system of analysis. Here we have three times two blue candlesticks with two red candlesticks of correction in between. The last blue candlestick implies a correction to be followed, which then appears in the following three red candlesticks.

In chart 4.7, box A shows us three blue candlesticks. As the third candlestick breaks the Kijun, we expect a test of this break with a red candlestick. This occurs even if the candlestick finishes blue on close. It will be included with the following two red candlesticks to give our count of three.

Chart 4.7: Three candlesticks

I will note in passing here that it is important to know how this red/blue candlestick was built. For example, on a five-minute time frame, it might be seen that it was red for 4 minutes and 30 seconds, and that it was only over the final 30 seconds that it switched to blue. This is important because the first part gives us the true colour of the candlestick (red in this case), and then it tells us that the Kijun breakout bullish movement is valid and will have an interesting profit potential. We are therefore confident that price will go to the cloud.

Box B gives us three blue candlesticks but with three correction candlesticks in the middle. Then three blue candlesticks end the movement at the target bottom of the cloud.

Box C shows the case where the candlesticks are only counted from the break of one level, here the Kijun, which is crossed downwards. It is a signal for the reversal of trend, and therefore we only consider the candlestick that represents this information. The previous red candlestick is not significant as it makes a low point higher than the previous blue and it closes on the Tenkan. In other words, it's a neutral candlestick.

On the other hand, in box D, the breakout candle of the SSB is taken into account because it is the colour of the current trend and this crossing is a confirmation of the movement (the Lagging Span validates the move by breaking its Kijun). We have three reds followed by a corrective blue.

Box E also gives three red candlesticks; the small blue ones not being significant.

Finally, there are a few special cases with two hesitation candlesticks in circle F: these are taken as a single candlestick because they are identical and they make higher highs and higher lows. So they could be replaced by a single blue candle.

The blue candlestick in circle G is not taken into account because its blue part remains under the Tenkan and does not validate a price increase. In addition, two red candlesticks were present just before. Thus, a bearish bias is maintained. Only the next candlestick, by the break of his Tenkan, validates its colour and will be the first of the three that corrects to the SSB of the cloud.

Finally, circle H has both a blue candlestick of correction after the three reds (shadow) and a red candlestick (Doji tombstone) of a continuation bearish pattern and thus the first red candlestick of the series of three to come. The lower point above the third red is the signal of the next blue.

Through these few examples (that are far from exhaustive), I hope you will understand the importance of reading the **formation** of candlesticks. As trading is active, you must read the market dynamically.

Let's now look at how to use this analysis for managing positions.

Entering the market

To avoid being in a correction contrary to the direction of the initial position, do not enter on a third candlestick even if there is acceleration. The following candlestick will be of opposite colour and it will allow us to enter a few points earlier, avoiding finding ourselves in negative territory because of the correction.

Exiting the market

In the case of an acceleration as soon as you see a third candlestick weakening in its power (which can be confirmed on lower time frames), it is better to exit, even if this involves getting back into the market when the correction is complete.

Playing a correction

On a signal given by a reversal candlestick, or on a key level reached, a position can be opened in the opposite direction of the trend and the movement played over three candlesticks by defining a precise correction target. As long as this series of three candlesticks is not finished, the correction will remain valid and we can keep the position until the target level is reached, or at the completion of the third candlestick.

But if the target is reached with three candlesticks and a fourth candlestick of the same colour starts and breaks this level, it is imperative to wait for the close of this candlestick because it can turn into a Doji and change colour by returning under the level.

Managing a delicate position

If you find yourself uncomfortably in a position opposite to the current price direction (due to bad analysis or an entry too early), it is wise to wait for the third candlestick followed by a candlestick in the direction opposite to the trade entered and then exit with a lower loss. This is valid for normal market movements, but not for accelerations which sometimes do not even allow to wait for the close of the candlestick.

Averaging a position

If the movement in three corrective candlesticks in which the trader has been caught (by entering too early, for example) is set for a particular target, to the completion of the third candlestick that validates this level, it is then possible to open a position of similar size to that first taken in order to reduce the amount of the unrealised loss. The fact that we have identified the end of this correction by its third candlestick makes it possible to have greater certainty that the trend of the initial movement will resume. Finally, let's look at a case study.

Chart 4.8: USDCHF

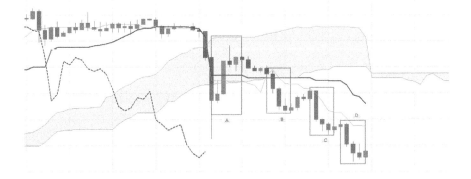

A) As soon as the long red candlestick starts to rise, we can enter a long position on the premise that the market will test the strong exit of the cloud. And we exit on the third blue candlestick which ends in a red Doji.

B) We become a seller on the break of the Kijun, this red candlestick having been blocked by the Tenkan. We exit then on the third candlestick. The correction is made in three blue candlesticks that get blocked on the Tenkan.

C) We sell again, and exit on the third red. Let correction continue.

D) Another sell, and exit on the third red.

This is a way of trading that is only valid for a very aggressive short-term trader. Each correction being an opportunity to reposition a little higher than the exit point and thus a chance to grab a few extra points.

But it is also interesting on longer time frames because it avoids the corrections and also secures profits, by contrast a stop-loss always loses part of the gains.

Regarding these examples, it goes without saying that these three-candlestick moves are for trending markets, i.e. they are not appropriate in undecided markets or those in consolidation.

In order to better identify these configurations and to validate their counts, it is imperative to observe the formation of each candlestick and to understand its meaning. I really insist on this idea that it's necessary to *be in* the market, *to live and feel it*. All the indicators that can be added on the chart are only there to help confirm one's feeling about the market psychology and enable one to build a strategy in accordance with this feeling.

It's with this idea of making easier the process of decision-making that Goichi Hosoda developed Ichimoku as a complement to the reading of candlesticks, giving the technical elements essential to the development of a strategy.

We will next see how to exploit the information given by candlesticks and Ichimoku in order to develop trading strategies.

Trading with Ichimoku as the only indicator

As explained in the previous chapters, Ichimoku's power comes from the fact that it takes into account an extended period of time through the calculation of its different lines. The Lagging Span represents the market's memory while the Tenkan and the Kijun indicate momentum behind current price action. Finally, the future is illustrated by the cloud. With one single chart, these three time periods necessary for understanding the market studied are clearly visible.

In the same manner, it's really important to be able to read charts in different periods of time when developing trading strategies. The way to do this is simple:

shuffle between three different time frames, all focusing on the one upon which the trading strategy is based.

The trading style with Ichimoku that I am now going to detail is the one that I adopt every day for my own personal account.

Choosing the currency pair to trade

I start each trading session by opening my charts with the eight currency pairs that I follow on a regular basis. For all pairs, I work with 240-minute charts except for the USDCHF which I trade and use as an indicator of the US dollar via a daily chart. I chose this time frame because it gives me a decent perspective for both intraday and swing trading strategies. Furthermore, this time frame in particular gives very effective trading signals with Ichimoku. It also allows for a better understanding of the previous day's price action by breaking daily candlesticks into six separate periods.

So, on my computer screen, I look at each of the miniature charts to identify trading opportunities while focusing on the position of prices with respect to their Kijun. Since Kijun breaks are what provide trading signals, I mark these levels on each currency pair in order to be able to keep track of it on higher or lower time frames according to the duration of my trading plan.

Chart 4.9: Multi-screen analysis

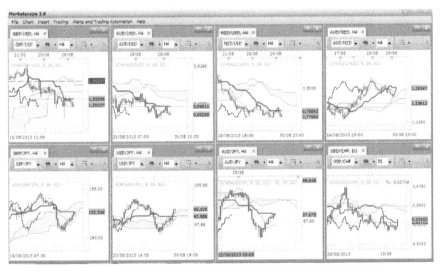

In the above example (chart 4.9), three currency pairs seem worth a closer look: AUDNZD, GBPJPY and AUDJPY. **These pairs are likely to break their Kijuns before the end of the day.** Next, I examine the likelihood of a Kijun break in relation to the cloud and the upside potential. AUDNZD shows a possible move higher without any obstacles in the way apart from the Lagging Span that may be hindered by prices. I choose this pair for a trade that will last a couple of days.

Chart 4.10: AUDNZD (Australian dollar/New Zealand dollar)

GBPJPY is more complicated as prices are facing two resistances (SSB in line with the Kijun and SSA) and the Lagging Span will have to overcome its own Kijun before confronting prices and then the Tenkan. I will only choose this pair for a very short period of time to make profit between the different resistance levels.

Chart 4.11: GBPJPY (pound sterling/Japanese yen) 240-minute chart

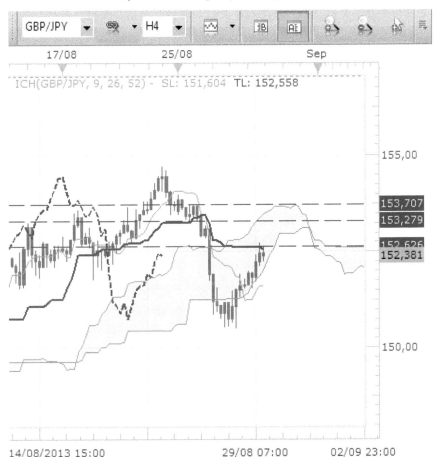

As for the AUDJPY cross, it is a transitional stage with well-defined short-term trade opportunities and a potential bullish development over the medium term. So, after a Kijun break, prices will only have two resistances left, the last of which is the thin cloud which may give in easily. The biggest obstacles are for the Lagging Span, which will need to be watched closely. It is this line that will either validate or nullify any technical breaks observed in price action.

Chart 4.12: AUDJPY (Australian dollar/Japanese yen) 240-minute chart

So, I will select the two first pairs that I will subsequently analyse over longer time frames in order to determine overall trends and identify each one's potential.

Analysis and strategic planning of trades

Example 1: AUDNZD (Australian dollar/New Zealand dollar)

AUDNZD is the currency pair that seems to offer the highest potential gain. I'll first start with the **monthly** chart in order to get an idea of the market's prevailing trend.

Chart 4.13: AUDNZD, monthly chart

Prices are in a bearish trend below the cloud but have pared losses a bit since the beginning of the current month. The first bullish target is at the SSB situated above the Lagging Span. This is the only Ichimoku element that is liable to pose an obstacle to prices, which are cleared to continue rising all the way to the Tenkan or even the Kijun/SSB double resistance. As such, the potential profit from this trade, which would last several months, is very attractive. The stop-loss would be trailed higher up to each resistance broken by prices as they rally towards the ultimate target area.

Here, the idea is to enter in a counter trend which offers significant gains.

However, every time a target (resistance) is reached and validated by sending prices down, a selling position could be entered to get back in the initial falling trend.

This style of trading (trend and counter trend) enables the trader to capitalise twice: first by playing against the trend but with well-defined stop-loss and targets, and second by reversing the position in the trend as soon as a target reached sends a reversal signal.

This double type of trading prevents waiting during a correction in the trend, above all on long-term time frames.

Looking at the **weekly** chart, a break above the Tenkan would convince me to enter the market as a buyer as soon as prices close above the Tenkan. This signal has not yet been given. Monthly resistances are shown on this chart, one of which corresponds with the weekly Kijun. This is the first price target that I will keep in this strategy.

Chart 4.14: AUDNZD, weekly chart

Lastly, prices have started to change direction on the **daily** chart after having broken the Kijun, which is validated by the bullish monthly candlestick. The yet-to-be confirmed bullish reversal (counter trend) is evident in the current weekly candlestick. So, no contradiction can be found between these different time frames. Shuffling among different charts simply allows more in-depth analysis of each candlestick for the next higher time frame. On all three charts just seen, the trend is without a doubt bearish as prices are trading below their respective clouds.

Chart 4.15: AUDNZD, daily chart

This breakdown leads me to focus on the currency pair's upcoming price action as the expected move higher unfolds and will allow me to profit from these trend discrepancies in various time frames by taking positions over different periods of time.

Initially, I will enter the market as a swing trader because holding a position over a longer period of time will allow me to optimise potential profit relative to the limited risk taken. On the daily chart, chart 4.15, so long as the Tenkan plays its role as support, I will remain long in the market and with the hope of seeing the currency pair cross the cloud to the upside. Note that such an event would occur at the same time as the Kijun break by the Lagging Span.

Then I will add to my position in order to trade the second movement between the cloud's SSB and the monthly target.

So, my strategy on this time frame is the following:

- Initiate 50% of the position above the Tenkan.
- Place a stop-loss below the Kijun to avoid a brief dip below the Tenkan in the event that prices retest the latter, and more precisely below the level formed by the two horizontal Tenkan lines.

- Exit the trade at the SSB level if prices do not confirm the bullish potential beyond this point, or trail the stop higher just below this level in order to hold on to the position.
- If prices and the Lagging Span confirm the bullish trend change, add the other 50% of the remaining position above the SSB. A stop-loss will be placed ten or so points below the monthly level that is also shown on the weekly chart.

Should this short-term bullish trend be validated with prices crossing the cloud in this time frame, the monthly bearish trend won't be negated.

Executing trades and managing stop-losses

At this point, I refine the entry execution by following price action on the 240- and 60-minute charts.

Chart 4.16: AUDNZD, 240- and 60-minute charts

The trade will be entered upon a break above the Kijun on the 240-minute chart. The 60-minute chart gives me a chance to study price action in detail: the Doji that took shape beneath the Kijun on the 240-minute chart is due to the Lagging Span failing to validate the rally on the 60-minute chart. Prices have fallen back below the cloud and may continue lower to test the Kijun. If the latter gives in to selling pressure, I will drop this particular entry strategy because this will mean a break below the Tenkan on the 240-minute chart on top of the Lagging Span falling towards its Kijun. The upwards correction will come to an end as the overall bearish trend identified on the monthly chart reasserts itself.

Watching the 60- and 240-minute charts allows me to place a relatively tight stop in order to exit the market quickly when it moves in the opposite direction initially expected. Since the 240-minute chart is that primarily used for trading with Ichimoku, whether it be for intraday strategies or swing positions, my ultimate trading signal is given once prices have closed above the Kijun in this time frame. Here, I still do not have a bullish entry signal, so if prices end up falling below the 60-minute Kijun, I will abandon the trade. My stop-loss is thus close by and placed just below the Kijun. I widen it in higher time frames when the trade is in the correct direction.

It goes without saying that it is better to place a **technical stop** and to adjust the size of the position in accordance with the principles of money management than to base it on a financial amount of loss and to have a stop that is inconsistent with the market.

My stops are always based on the technical but are adjusted depending on the time frame used for entering positions as well as the market's progression.

So, as I have already stated, my stop is tight at the beginning of the trade, becomes larger during the intermediate progression of the market and is again tight once the final target is within close reach. Many traders trail their stops to their entry price. In my opinion, this is a mistake. Certainly, no losses occur if the stop is hit; but no profit is realised either as the trade is exited. If the stop remains at a consistent technical level corresponding with the invalidation of an expected market move, it will not be hit if prices end up going in the anticipated direction. **A stop that is not based on technical is doomed to failure.** As a result, I always trail stops as soon as new technical levels arise.

With Ichimoku, I rely on:

- The Kijun, especially at the start of the trade because the position is initiated when prices break it. A break in the other direction will invalidate the signal first given.

- An SSB that is overcome in the middle of a move by the market. Since this line is robust, traders should trade it in the same manner as with the Kijun.

- Finally, the Tenkan – in particular at the end of the trade – as it gives an alert on the end of the movement. When prices are close to the final target and break the Tenkan, this indicates that the market's move is over and that it is wise to close the trade.

Thus, my stops are rarely hit and only in the case of an invalidation by the market. Another example of how to place a stop-loss is presented on page 122 with a trade on AUDUSD.

Example 2: with the other currency pair selected on lower time frames: AUDJPY

I start with the same approach to analysing this currency pair by looking at the **weekly** chart (chart 4.17): the trend is bearish ever since prices fell below the Kijun. The Lagging Span validates this by equally breaking below its Kijun. It is interesting to note that prices have found support at the 61.8% Fibonacci level, which is in agreement with the cloud's SSB.

Chart 4.17: AUDJPY, weekly chart

Two scenarios are to be considered:

- prices keep falling towards the 76.4%/78.6% Fibonacci level, or
- a double bottom is in progress, which would mean that a break above 90 yen would trigger a buy signal with a target at 96 yen (Kijun level).

On the **daily** chart (chart 4.18), strong resistance is provided by the Kijun that is in line with the flattened SSB to the right. A break above this level would be considered a strong buy signal. On the other hand, if this resistance continues to hold, prices will likely consolidate laterally in the direction of the flattened cloud. The pair could end in a range-bound between the resistance and the double bottom level for several days.

However, prices will probably fall further if they do not rise immediately above the Tenkan. There is therefore no alert as to the end of the bearish trend that is well in place.

Finally, the trend line drawn on the chart is a possible obstacle to any rally in the market.

Chart 4.18: AUDJPY, daily chart

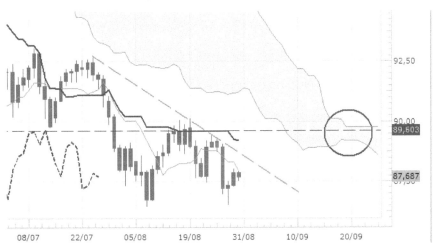

Upon looking at these two charts, I realise that the direction in which one should trade is not clear. For a trend-follower, it would be wiser to wait for prices to exit the weekly cloud downwards, to be confirmed by the Tenkan and trend line resistance on the daily time frame.

Otherwise, a short-term position could be initiated to take some profits from this break in the bearish trend.

Indeed, on the **240-minute chart**, chart 4.19, it is possible to enter long on the short term between the perfectly-defined levels, provided that prices break above the Kijun.

Chart 4.19: AUDJPY, 240-minute chart

I proceed by planning my strategies via a 60-minute chart (chart 4.20).

Chart 4.20: AUDJPY, 60-minute chart

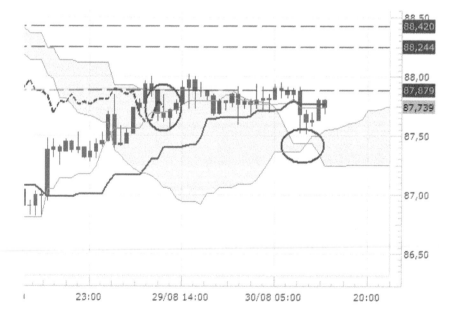

Prices attempt to break above the double resistance after having held above the cloud twist, which would have led to a strong fall in the market. Given this, I would rather look for an opportunity to buy the pair with the following strategy:

- Initiate the trade above 87.879 yen.
- Stop-loss at 87.53 yen.
- Targets at 88.244, 88.420 and 88.785 as indicated on the 240-minute chart.

At the same time, I notice that prices are now above a double support. The direction of the trade taken on this currency pair will depend on whether the market closes below or above this support.

I go ahead and plan an alternative strategy with a bearish bias this time:

- Enter the market below the double resistance at 87.71 yen.
- Stop-loss at 87.879 yen.
- Targets: the first is positioned at the point at which the Lagging Span meets its Kijun (87.38 yen), which is also the SSB at the cloud twist. The second target is found at the cloud's SSB level, or 87.227 yen.

Next, as for managing the position, a new analysis will need to be done for each level that is reached in order to determine whether or not the trade should be closed or if the position should be added to.

To do this, I examine the way in which prices reach each support/resistance: in which time frame; the candlestick's size; economic releases; and how the market reacts at the technical level. In this type of market study, shuffling between different time frames is essential. Personal intuition and knowledge of the asset is also a factor.

Finally, I fine-tune the entry with the help of a **15-minute chart** (chart 4.21).

Chart 4.21: AUDJPY, 15-minute chart

Prices are stuck between the Kijun and the SSB; the Lagging Span is advancing within the cloud. The currency pair is obviously in an area of uncertainty without any clear direction. I choose to wait for a signal, which is given seven candlesticks later.

Chart 4.22: AUDJPY, 15-minute chart

Take note of the precision with which prices stop falling on each support identified on the hourly chart. This chart is updated in chart 4.23.

Chart 4.23: AUDJPY, 60-minute chart

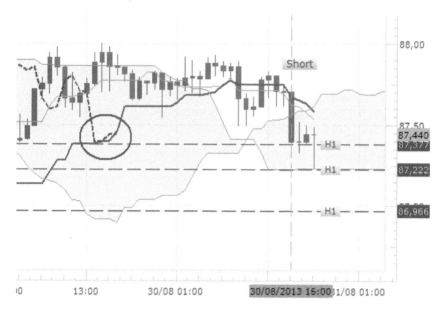

After testing the second target, prices quickly rise back above the first, leading the Lagging Span to bounce off its Kijun thus negating for a while the fall.

The trade was closed via a limit order because the fact that the market tested the first support for such a long time on the 15-minute chart was a reason to be more cautious in expecting further declines in prices. One could only hope for a brief acceleration downwards, which did indeed occur. This is why it is a good idea to place such limit orders in order to promptly close out trades.

The currency pair should now move higher towards the Kijun/Tenkan double resistance. This rebound in prices should not be traded as it would imply a risk/reward ratio less than one and above all because it would be against the trend.

The following conclusion can be made on this trade: if prices are trading in an area of uncertainty like in the charts just shown, traders can either stay out of the market or they can establish strategies in both directions (bullish and bearish) and rely on small time frames in order to determine as soon as possible which trade will be executed.

Very short-term trading

This kind of trading is really hard to explain in a book because it is necessary to take a lot of screenshots of three or four different time frames all at the same time in order to explain a train of thought that has to be as fast as possible.

So, I will try to show you the **basic principles** of short-term trading through several examples.

Whether one opts for an intraday trading strategy or a swing position, the analysis and decision-making process remains the same. The main difference lies in the need to shuffle between several charts throughout the entirety of the trade. Five-minute candlesticks require much more attention than hourly ones.

Some traders call this type of trading scalping. I prefer to call it very short-term (VST) trading because I aim for more than just two or three points per trade. In the currency markets, I do not trade unless I expect to be able to make at least 15 to 20 points of profit. As it is crucial to verify a technical break's validity in VST trading lest ending up stopped out of the market with a loss, traders must wait much longer before entering the market. This means that I forego several points of potential profit before initiating such a trade.

Ichimoku is extremely efficient when it comes to trading on shorter time frames, but the rules to be followed are much stricter. Any hastiness or exemption often results in a quick loss. This indicator's simplicity and precision are major advantages when entering the market or making quick decisions. Each line's value should also be taken immediately into account during the analysis process.

Here are three examples that illustrate VST trading strategies. The first is with 15-minute, 5-minute and 1-minute charts. The second, which does not succeed, uses the 15-minute and 5-minute time frames. The last example is of an economic release in the United Kingdom.

Example 1: GBPUSD

Quite often, VST trades arise from opportunities to enter the market when prices are retracing within a larger trend that in this case is ignored. Range-bound markets in which prices fluctuate between different technical levels are also good examples of VST trade opportunities. In such setups, one only seeks to make a few points of profit with a larger position size to compensate for the limited variation in prices traded.

Chart 4.24: GBPUSD, 240- and 60-minute charts

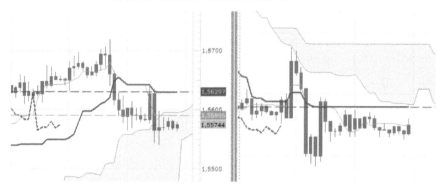

In the **240-minute chart** (left), prices are trading within the cloud, signalling market equilibrium and uncertainty regarding the future trend. The Lagging Span has not validated the fall in prices as it remains currently above its Kijun.

The **60-minute chart** (right) confirms the lack of direction in the market. That said, the last candlestick attempted to rise above the Tenkan. This may foreshadow a possible test of the Kijun further up. I can therefore look to enter the market upon a break of the Tenkan with a stop just below it and a target established at the Kijun. I would not aim any higher because the thick cloud is likely to block prices.

I go ahead and fine-tune my entry by using the **15- and 5-minute** charts.

Chart 4.25: GBPUSD, 15- and 5-minute charts

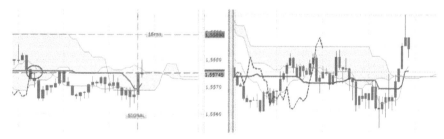

A buy signal is given in the 15-minute chart (left) with the candlestick that has pierced through the cloud, broken the Kijun and closed at the same level as this line. Following this, prices have attempted to rise completely above the cloud but have fallen back within it, closing at practically the same level as the previous candlestick's closing price. Twice, the Lagging Span has failed to break its Kijun: the buy signal has not yet been fully validated.

In the 5-minute chart (right), the signal can be seen with the Kijun break and prices that have stopped rising at the SSB level. The Lagging Span is currently above this level.

The bearish engulfing pattern in the 5-minute chart suggests that prices may continue falling towards the Tenkan and the Kijun. This would correspond with prices pulling back to test the Kijun in the 15-minute chart.

In order to verify that this expected decline is really possible, I can take a quick look at the 1-minute chart: the Kijun currently provides support to prices.

Chart 4.26: GBPUSD, 1-minute chart

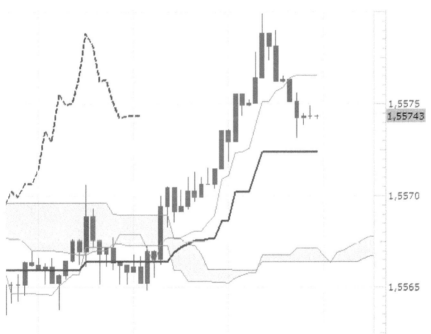

Accordingly, this level needs to give in to selling pressure in order to see a further fall in prices.

Chart 4.27: GBPUSD, 1-minute chart

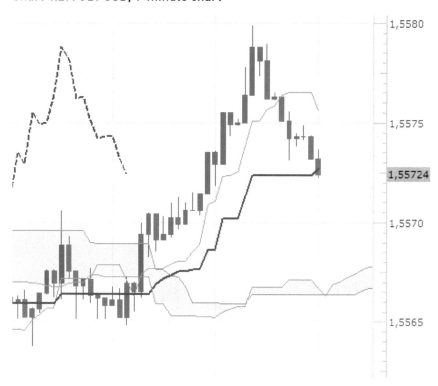

Prices close on the Kijun then break it, opening the way to a test of the supports in the 15- and 5-minute charts (below).

Chart 4.28: GBPUSD, 15- and 5-minute charts

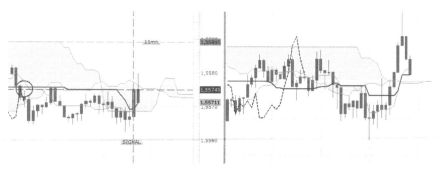

Chart 4.29: GBPUSD, 15- and 5-minute charts

Then they rebound. I get ready to take position as soon as prices rise above 1.55749 in the 15-minute chart, corresponding with the SSB in the 5-minute time frame.

Chart 4.30: GBPUSD, 15- and 5-minute charts

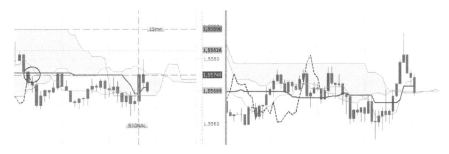

Unfortunately, the market continues to fall. I end up doing nothing and wait to see what happens next.

Chart 4.31: GBPUSD, 15- and 5-minute charts

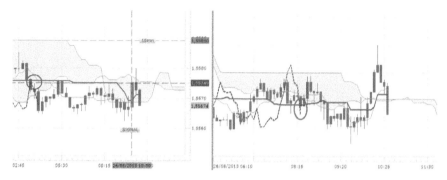

In both the 5- and 15-minute charts, prices break below their respective clouds. The 5-minute Lagging Span also breaks its Kijun.

At this point, I now have a sell signal validated by the Lagging Span in both time frames. The buy strategy can therefore be abandoned. But I decide to wait for the current candlesticks to close to fully invalidate the bullish scenario and look to short the currency pair.

Chart 4.32: GBPUSD, 15- and 5-minute charts

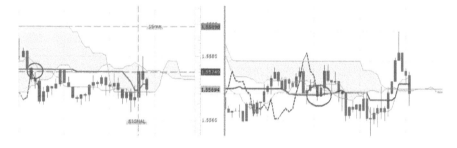

In what follows, the candlesticks start to rebound. I am still waiting to see how they close.

Chart 4.33: GBPUSD, 15- and 5-minute charts

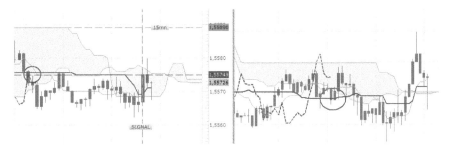

In both time frames, the candlesticks end up closing above their respective Kijuns, thereby invalidating the sell signal during this period. This demonstrates a critical point when trading with Ichimoku: **always wait for the current candlestick to close**.

Chart 4.34: GBPUSD, 1-minute chart

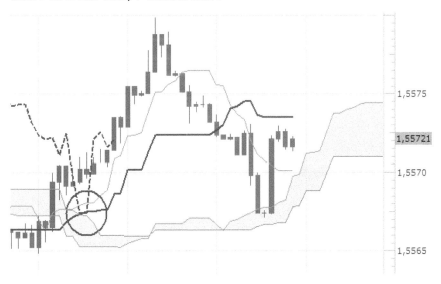

As prices seem to have stopped falling in the middle of nowhere in the 15- and 5-minute charts, when I look at the 1-minute chart I see that the Lagging Span marked the end to this decline by rebounding off its Kijun. This illustrates a second important rule: **always keep these three time frames in front of you throughout the trade**.

Chart 4.35: GBPUSD, 15- and 5-minute charts

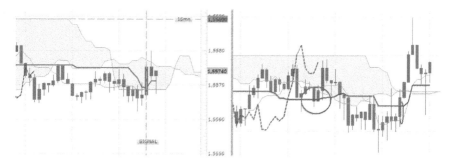

Now prices start to rise again. I get ready to enter the market at the same level as before. As this currency pair is volatile, I do not enter in anticipation even though the latest signals are in the direction of my initial trade. Thus the third rule: **do not anticipate future price movements just to book a few more points** (2–3 pips) of profit at the risk of winding up on the wrong side of the market. In this case here, on top of this currency pair's natural volatility, one must not forget that prices have just attempted to break lower. Nothing is keeping them from doing this again.

Chart 4.36: GBPUSD, 15- and 5-minute charts

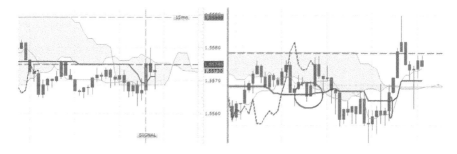

What happens next in the above charts is an example of this: prices do not succeed in rallying to the expected buy level. A further rise in prices is not guaranteed.

Chart 4.37: GBPUSD, 15- and 5-minute charts

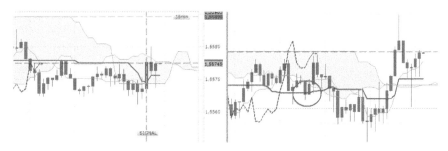

The market starts rallying again, and I initiate a buy position just above the level previously identified (the 15-minute Kijun and the 5-minute SSB).

Chart 4.38: GBPUSD, 15- and 5-minute charts

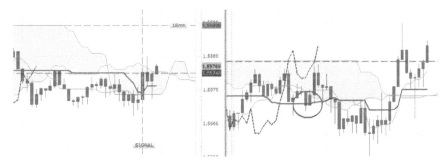

The order is executed and I am now in a long position. I still have the same price target – the 15-minute SSB which is also the Kijun in the 60-minute chart – and the stop-loss is placed below the 15-minute Kijun used for the entry.

Chart 4.39: GBPUSD, 1-minute chart

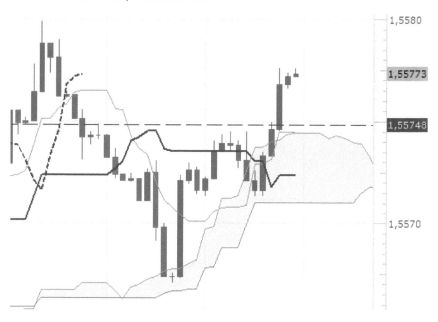

A quick look at the 1-minute chart shows that the move is weakening, but the Lagging Span to the left has a nearby support with its Tenkan.

Chart 4.40: GBPUSD, 1-minute chart

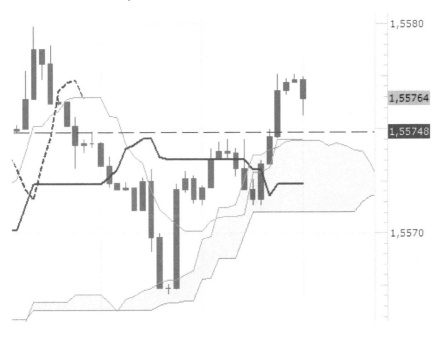

This support holds, and prices do not end up falling back to my entry level. The rally should continue now as this is so far only a pause in the market.

The brief correction seen in the 5-minute chart (chart 4.41) is reassuring because the Lagging Span is still above the cloud and prices well beyond the Tenkan, which has an upward slope.

Chart 4.41: GBPUSD, 5-minute chart

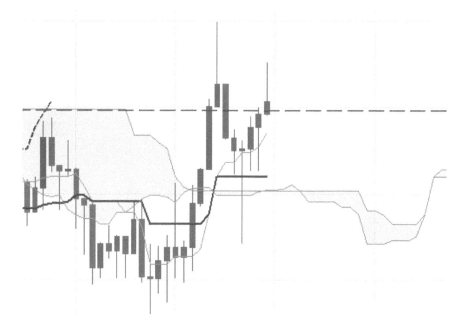

Coming back to the 15- and 5-minute charts, the rally is engaged. Now I start getting ready for the moment to close out the position.

Chart 4.42: GBPUSD, 15- and 5-minute charts

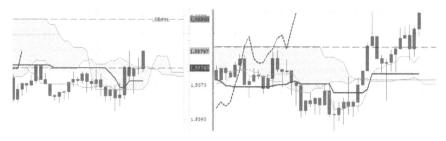

The move higher accelerates, bringing prices practically to my target. I exit the trade as I prefer to forego a few points rather than see the market fall back to my entry price, which could happen just as fast as the rally did.

Chart 4.43: GBPUSD, 15- and 5-minute charts

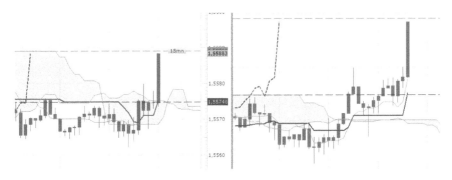

What follows next shows me that I was right to close my trade.

Chart 4.44: GBPUSD, 15- and 5-minute charts

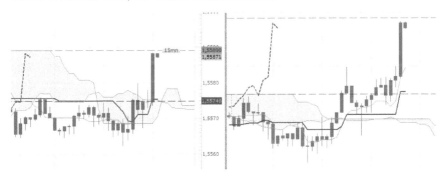

Chart 4.45 shows the end of the movement in the 240- and 60-minute charts. In the 240-minute time frame (left), prices rose to test the Tenkan on top of a bearish trend line. Likewise, in the 60-minute chart (right), prices test the Kijun again but the cloud resistance is much too thick. Prices will start to fall again.

Chart 4.45: GBPUSD, 240- and 60-minute charts

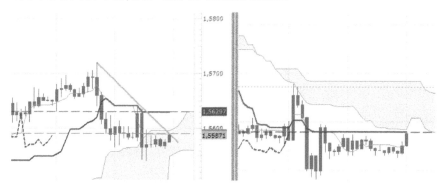

Chart 4.46: GBPUSD, 240- and 60-minute charts

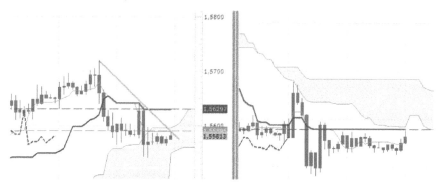

This trade presented an opportunity to make 35 points of profit with one single 15-minute candlestick, but with an hour's worth of waiting prior to taking position. VST trading requires sharp analysis and the patience to wait for all necessary confirmation before entering the market. Ichimoku is a particularly efficient tool in this type of trading provided that all rules stated in this example are followed. This can certainly make traders wait for a while, but the results will eventually be there.

Example 2: NZDUSD (New Zealand dollar/US dollar)

Chart 4.47: NZDUSD, 240-minute chart

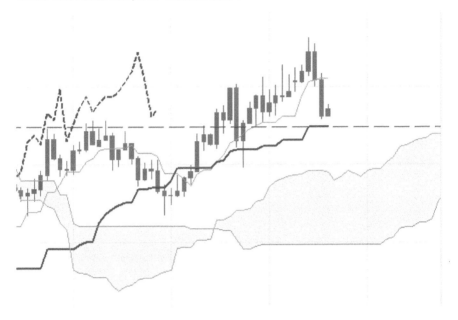

Looking at this 240-minute chart (chart 4.47), prices have not yet reached the Kijun but seem to want to start rising again. The overall trend being bullish, it is possible to expect the currency pair to rise back to the Tenkan and even rally further above it, thereby invalidating the bearish alert.

Chart 4.48: NZDUSD, 60-minute chart

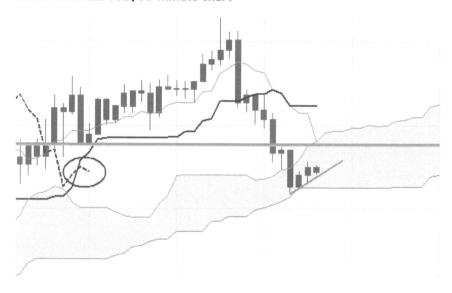

In the 60-minute chart (chart 4.48), prices are rebounding off the cloud SSB, but the Lagging Span has crossed its Kijun, validating the fall in prices. The Tenkan is plunging towards the cloud (SSA) bringing down the level of resistance. A corrective move with three candlesticks is in progress with the upside of the cloud as target. This double resistance should push prices lower. A downward move would therefore be initiated upon a break below the SSB currently below prices. The currency pair would in this case fall as far as the 240-minute Kijun.

Chart 4.49: NZDUSD, 60-minute chart

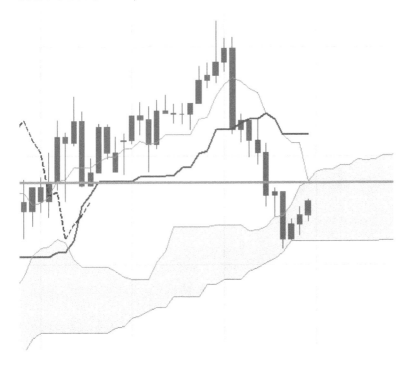

Prices continue rising towards resistance (chart 4.49).

Chart 4.50: NZDUSD, 15-minute chart

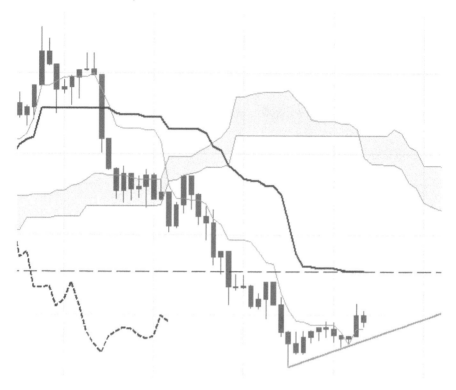

In the 15-minute chart (chart 4.50), prices have broken above the Tenkan and have pulled back on this level as a classic test of a breakout. They should test the Kijun, which is at the same level as the Tenkan in the 60-minute chart. This is the target of this position.

Chart 4.51: NZDUSD, 5-minute chart

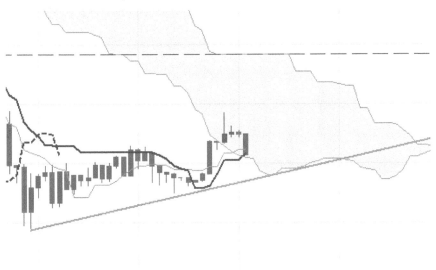

The next 5-minute chart (chart 4.51) details the last movement seen in the 15-minute time frame. I may expect prices to rebound here as they are testing three supports: the Tenkan and the Kijun, both close by, and the cloud SSA. Take note of the trend line reinforcing the cloud's lower edge as well as the Lagging Span, which should find support on the top of past candlesticks in line with the Tenkan. It may well break above the Kijun again to validate bullish price action.

The bullish scenario mentioned in the 240-minute time frame is therefore worth considering at this moment.

Chart 4.52: NZDUSD, 15-minute chart

15 minutes (chart 4.52): the Tenkan acts as support.

Notice that the Lagging Span is of no interest whatsoever in this time frame as it is far from prices. We can therefore ignore it for the time being.

Chart 4.53: NZDUSD, 5-minute chart

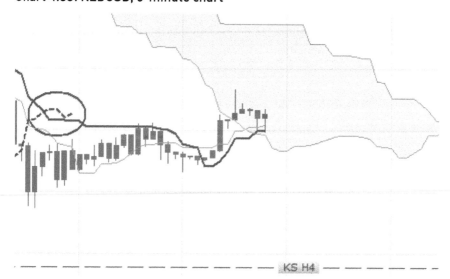

5 minutes (chart 4.53): the Lagging Span has risen back above the Kijun, validating once again the bullish movement in the market. Prices are rebounding above their triple support. This is the entry level for a long position with a stop placed below the support.

Chart 4.54: NZDUSD, 15-minute chart

15 minutes (chart 4.54): prices continue rising towards the Kijun.

Chart 4.55: NZDUSD, 5-minute chart

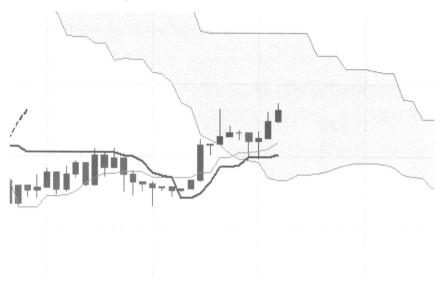

5 minutes (chart 4.55): pursuit of bullish price action.

Chart 4.56: NZDUSD, 15-minute chart

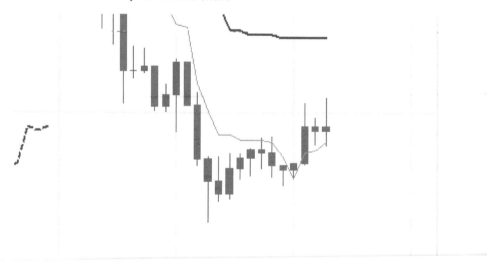

15 minutes (chart 4.56): prices pare gains but the Tenkan remains intact.

Chart 4.57: NZDUSD, 5-minute chart

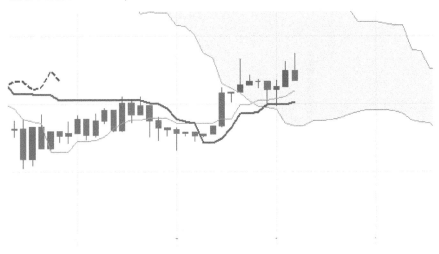

5 minutes (chart 4.57): the spread between the Tenkan and the Kijun widens, meaning that short-term momentum is picking up.

Chart 4.58: NZDUSD, 5-minute chart

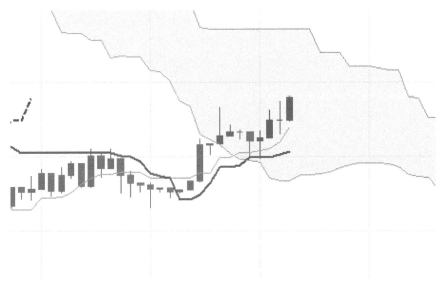

5 minutes (chart 4.58): prices take off again, and the Tenkan slope increases.

Chart 4.59: NZDUSD, 15-minute chart

15 minutes (chart 4.59): the resumption of bullish price action is now evident in this time frame.

Chart 4.60: NZDUSD, 5-minute chart

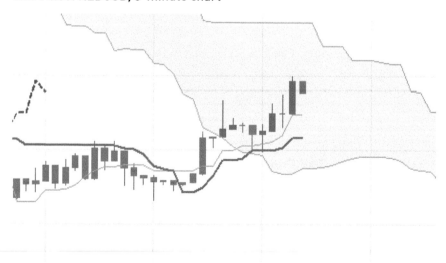

5 minutes (chart 4.60): possible pullback to the Tenkan.

Chart 4.61: NZDUSD, 15-minute chart

15 minutes (chart 4.61): a key movement is taking shape in this time frame: the Kijun (my target) has suddenly edged lower. The amount of pips that I was hoping to book on this trade has just been reduced, and the fact that this line has resumed its decline is an alert as to the longevity of the bullish movement. The Tenkan needs to be watched as a return below it would signal the end of the bullish price movement.

Chart 4.62: NZDUSD, 5-minute chart

5 minutes (chart 4.62): the target revised downwards was almost reached, and the Doji signals a reversal. Prices have now pulled back to test the Tenkan without breaking below it. So, there is not yet any alert, but the position will be closed once the Tenkan is broken without waiting for the next candlestick to close below it. The bearish signal given by the market is reliable enough and may lead to increased selling pressure below the Tenkan.

Chart 4.63: NZDUSD, 5-minute chart

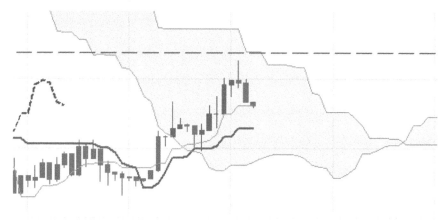

5 minutes (chart 4.63): prices are in the midst of breaking the Tenkan. The long position is closed. The Kijun provides the next support.

Chart 4.64: NZDUSD, 5-minute chart

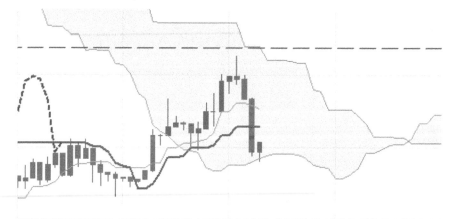

5 minutes (chart 4.64): prices have now broken below the Kijun. A bearish signal is given, confirmed by the Lagging Span which is back below its Kijun. The pre-empted exit strategy was appropriate.

Chart 4.65: NZDUSD, 15-minute chart

15 minutes (chart 4.65): the strong fall in the market results in prices breaking below the Tenkan in this time frame. A bearish alert is given, but one should wait for prices to continue falling below the short-term trend line before eventually entering short.

Chart 4.66: NZDUSD, 5- and 15-minute charts

5 minutes (chart 4.66, left): prices rise back above the Kijun, invalidating the signal previously given.

15 minutes (chart 4.66, right): the trend line holds, and prices cross back above the Tenkan to cancel the bearish alert.

Chart 4.67: NZDUSD, 5-minute chart

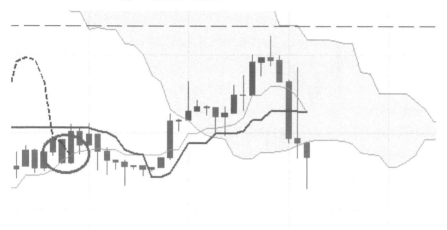

5 minutes (chart 4.67): eventually, the bearish movement resumes, and prices break below the cloud. As a logical result of this breakdown, the Lagging Span crosses prices as well as its Tenkan.

Chart 4.68: NZDUSD, 15-minute chart

15 minutes (chart 4.68): the trend line has been broken, and the overall bearish trend takes off again. A short-term sell position can be initiated with a target at the 240-minute Kijun.

This trade did not work out as originally planned since the price target was revised downwards when the Kijun ticked lower due to a mathematical result. Within the 26 periods taken into account for computing the mid-price, the prior correction suddenly entered the calculation due to the line's gradual rolling over to new candlesticks. The mid-price declined, leading the Kijun to tick downwards as the 26-period high dropped while the low remained unchanged.

So, it becomes clear that during the **planning phase of a strategy**, one has to make sure that the price target remains constant throughout the trade's estimated duration.

Here is a practical illustration of this:

Chart 4.69: Calculation of the target with the Kijun

The 26-period time span used in calculating the Kijun (space between the two grey dotted lines) moves progressively to the right. One can see that the mid-price will not change so long as the market does not hit a fresh high, which is shown with the candlestick on the red dotted line. At this precise point in time, the upper shadow of this candlestick is lower than the previous candlestick's high. And if prices do not hit fresh lows, the mid-price will fall. In counting the number of candlesticks, one can determine that the market has eight trading days to reach the established target without it being modified.

In the short term, this fact is most noticeable in the 15-minute chart. Over a longer period of time, the 240-minute chart shows this the best.

So, I consider these two time frames as being the most relevant for Ichimoku: they both provide the clearest signals via Kijun breakouts, the most plausible targets and the most precise information when it comes to actively following the position.

Of the three time frames used in establishing a trading strategy and managing live trades, these two are, depending on the investment horizon, at the centre of any analysis.

Below is a table that summarises the different time frames used according to the investment horizon of the strategy:

Investment horizon	Time frame 1	Time frame 2	Time frame 3
	Analysis	**Strategy**	**Position management**
Very short term	**15 minutes**	5 minutes	1 minute
Short term	60 minutes	**15 minutes**	5 minutes
Medium term	Daily	**240 minutes**	60 minutes
Long term	Weekly	Daily	**240 minutes**

It is often useful to consider another time frame higher than Time Frame 1 in order to have an idea as to the overall trend in the market. In the previous example, I first looked at the 240-minute chart before considering the lower time frames used in the trading strategy.

Example 3: GBPUSD and British economic releases

This example illustrates just how important Ichimoku's lines are even when faced with high volatility in the market.

Chart 4.70: 15- and 5-minute charts

15 minutes (chart 4.70, left): the market is hesitating around the Kijun, and the Lagging Span is advancing within the cloud (indication of neutrality).

5 minutes (chart 4.70, right): prices attempted twice to break above the cloud without success. Both the Tenkan and the Kijun are currently providing support. The Lagging Span has fallen back below the cloud and is heading towards its support.

Chart 4.71: 15- and 5-minute charts

15 minutes (chart 4.71, left): prices have begun to bounce off the Tenkan with precision.

5 minutes (chart 4.71, right): both prices and the Lagging Span are rebounding off their respective Kijuns.

Chart 4.72: 15- and 5-minute charts

15 minutes (chart 4.72, left): a new Kijun break is taking shape, and the Lagging Span is testing its price resistance.

5 minutes (chart 4.72, right): prices have broken above the cloud, but the Lagging Span has yet to do the same.

Chart 4.73: 15- and 5-minute charts

15 minutes (chart 4.73, left): the Lagging Span has failed to overcome its resistance, and prices have suddenly broken back below the Tenkan and the Kijun. This is the **market's reaction to the economic release**.

5 minutes (chart 4.73, right): the Lagging Span has been driven back by the SSA and is now testing the upper shadow of a candlestick just beneath the Tenkan. Prices have fallen back below the cloud and are breaking the Kijun.

Chart 4.74: 15- and 5-minute charts

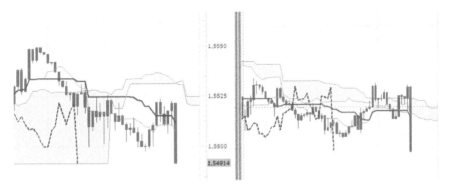

15 minutes (chart 4.74, left): the breakdown continues with the Lagging Span testing the cloud SSB.

5 minutes (chart 4.74, right): the Lagging Span crosses over prices, confirming the breakout to the downside. But given that this breakdown has occurred following an economic release, it is better to wait for the market to stabilise before planning to enter.

Chart 4.75: 15- and 5-minute charts

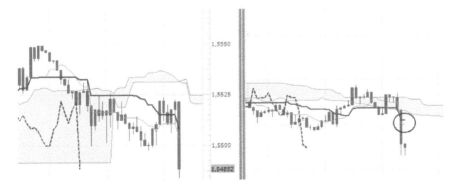

15 minutes (chart 4.75, left): the Lagging Span pierces the bottom of the cloud.

5 minutes (chart 4.75, right): the bearish movement comes to a halt as the Kijun flattens out.

Chart 4.76: 60- and 15-minute charts

60 minutes (chart 4.76, left): prices have held above the Kijun and have rebounded all the way to the Tenkan with the start of a new candlestick.

15 minutes (chart 4.76, right): the Lagging Span has come back inside the cloud and is rebounding off the SSB. Prices are currently testing the Tenkan/ Kijun double resistance.

Chart 4.77 shows the same price action in the 240-minute chart.

Chart 4.77: 240-minute chart

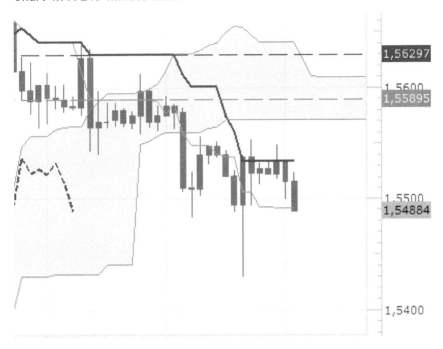

In this chart (4.77), prices are breaking below the Tenkan after multiple attempts to break above the Kijun.

Chart 4.78: 240-minute chart

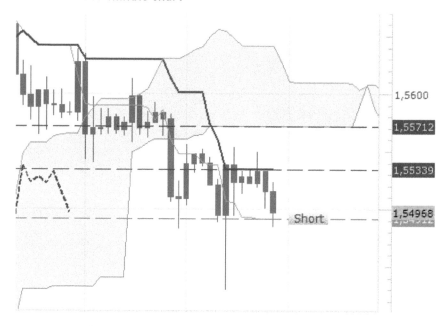

In the second chart (4.78), prices are stabilising above the Tenkan, thereby postponing the bearish signal.

Chart 4.79: 240-minute chart

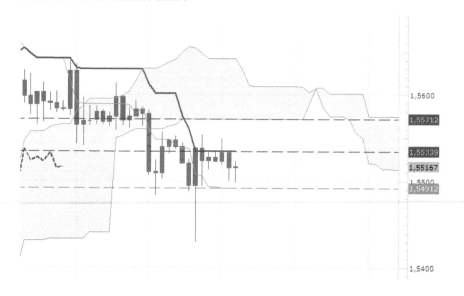

Finally, in the last chart (4.79), prices have continued to rise. A seventh test of the Kijun is likely. The economic release's effect has waned.

Example 4: AUDUSD (Australian dollar/US dollar)

A last example is a trade I followed live on Twitter.

A good intraday opportunity appears on looking at the daily chart (chart 4.80).

Chart 4.80: AUDUSD, daily chart

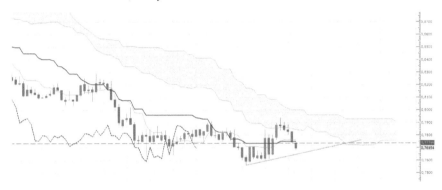

Prices confirm the break of the Kijun by falling further, and the Lagging Span is crossing its Tenkan. A bearish trend is taking place.

The first target to look for is the upside trend line. The strategy is thus to sell the continuation of this daily red candle.

Chart 4.81: AUDUSD, 240-minute chart

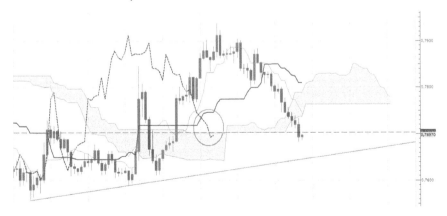

In the immediate inferior time frame 240-minute (chart 4.81), the bearish trend is confirmed with prices having crossed the thin cloud and the SSB as support. The Lagging Span has broken its Kijun and has entered its cloud.

Prices and the Lagging Span are both testing this breakout of the SSB. I wait for the validation of this test before selling.

Chart 4.82: AUDUSD, 60-minute chart

In the 60-minute time frame (chart 4.82), the pullback seems to be over with a test of the SSB by the first blue candle shadow and the second candle makes a lower high. **The trade is activated with a target a few points above the trend line.** The stop-loss is placed above the Tenkan. If prices happen to break the Tenkan on the upside, it could mean a move up to the Kijun thus setting the risk reward ratio at 1:3.

Chart 4.83: AUDUSD, 240-minute chart

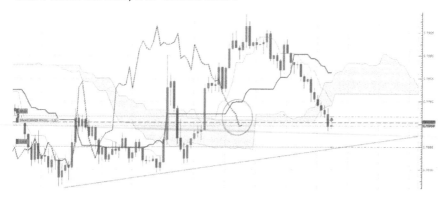

The candle body is shortening. And the stop-loss placed above the Tenkan on the 60-minute chart appears to be above the SSB on the 240-minute time frame, which is perfect (chart 4.83).

Chart 4.84: AUDUSD, 15-minute chart

In chart 4.84, a 15-minute chart, prices are range-bound and don't confirm the downside move expected.

On this chart, the stop-loss stands above the Kijun which is a perfect invalidation level on this time frame.

Time frames of 240-minute and 15-minute are of prime importance in Ichimoku so it's absolutely essential that the stop-loss level defined on the highest time frame is in perfect technical accordance on the lower time frames. Which is the case here: above the SSB (240-minute chart), above the Tenkan (60-minute chart) and above the Kijun (15-minute chart), different technical invalidation levels in accordance with each time frame considered.

Chart 4.85: AUDUSD, 5-minute chart

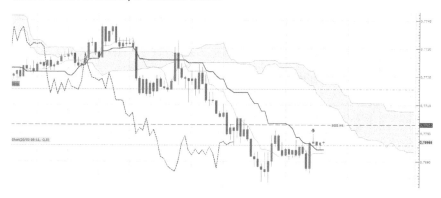

Looking at chart 4.85, the trade was entered on the shooting star, which is a 'reversal candlestick'. Even though it's not the top of a trend, it suggests that the correction of the downtrend could be over. Prices are above a double support Kijun plus Tenkan, which is not a good selling entry. But the trade was initiated on the 240-minute time frame. So this is just mere noise in the market on a very short-term basis. It means that when one enters a trade on a high time frame, it's not recommended to look at very low time frames.

This short time frame will just confirm the bearish strategy as soon as the double support is crossed. Note that the resistance level (H4 SSB) is well above the high of the 'shooting star'.

So the trade is still valid.

Chart 4.86: AUDUSD, 5-minute chart

Staying with the 5-minute in chart 4.86, the double support was finally broken with a strong red candlestick and the fall resumed perfectly followed by the Kijun.

Prices are close to a secondary trend line and the third originally red candlestick, but which turns out blue, is already pulling back from this level.

Chart 4.87: AUDUSD, 1-minute chart

AUD/USD (m1)

After looking at a 1-minute chart (chart 4.87), I consider that a correction is due very soon following the three red candlesticks.

Moreover, the gain is already of 32.5 pips, which is much more than the 25 pips I usually look for. So I decide to close the trade.

On a 1-minute chart, chart 4.87, you can follow the trade from entry to close. As seen earlier on a 5-minute chart, the entry is also wrong on this time frame. It should have been done on the candlestick in the right-hand red circle with the Lagging Span validating with a break below its Kijun and SSB (left-hand red circle). On the other hand, the close was well timed as prices moved higher just after. The following pips are just some points left to the market, with prices then beginning a consolidation that was rightly predicted by the Doji on the 5-minute chart (chart 4.88).

Chart 4.88: AUDUSD, 5-minute chart

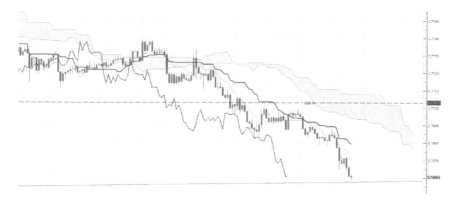

Having a quick look at the 15-minute time frame (chart 4.89) suggests I could have stayed longer as a third red candlestick was missing. This is the danger of watching at too short time frames, such as 1-minute or 5-minute, while having set a strategy on a higher time frame: here on the 240-minute time frame. One is caught in erratic price action of the market and closes the position before reaching the original target just by fear.

Chart 4.89: AUDUSD, 15-minute chart

Getting back to the time frame where the trade was entered, the 60-minute chart in chart 4.90, the close is perfectly done at the end of the third red candlestick. The few points missed on the very short time frame are just the shadow of the candle.

Chart 4.90: AUDUSD, 60-minute chart

AUD/USD (H1)

The next blue candlestick suggests that the fall could be over, confirmed by the Kijun and Tenkan getting flat.

Take note that the blue candlestick on which the trade was entered (see chart 4.82) turned out red at the end of the hour. It was the validation of the market resuming its downtrend.

The blue candlestick observed on the original chart (chart 4.82) ends only as the shadow of this 240-minute candle (chart 4.91). The target considered was almost reached. When one enters an automatic take profit, always leave a few extra points of profit in the market.

Chart 4.91: AUDUSD, 240-minute chart

AUD/USD (H4)

The red candlestick kept falling and the strategy was therefore judicious.

Chart 4.92: AUDUSD, daily chart

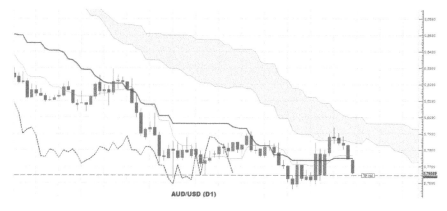

AUD/USD (D1)

To sum up this last example:

- When one establishes a strategy on a time frame longer than 60 minutes for an intraday trade, one must not watch charts below a 15-minute time frame as the noise in the market could make the trader close his position too early.
- A stop-loss set on a long time frame must be in technical accordance with a shorter time frame otherwise it may be executed due to the noise of the market.
- Finally, always leave a few points to the market in order to secure the gains.

The system consists of:

- Looking for potential profit in relation to technical levels. In this trade, the idea was to reach a support (trend line).
- Checking that the risk reward ratio is above 1:1.5, or better above 1:2. I personally take only trades with a risk reward ratio of 1:3.

Through these trading examples, one can see that Ichimoku gives traders good information that is reliable and precise no matter which time frame is studied.

Because one can easily and quickly move from one time frame to others – since there is no need to update parameters in different charts – Ichimoku's strong point is found in multi-temporal analysis. Traders are even more capable of understanding the way a given asset is traded and can better grasp market reactions. And keeping three different charts under constant surveillance allows them to refine entry and exit points, to better place technical stop-loss orders and to be aware of changes in price targets.

Three major and inescapable rules have been laid out in relation to this notion of time:

- **Know how to shuffle between different time frames** and to choose the three that are the most relevant throughout the duration of the trade.
- **Never pre-empt entry strategies**: one must above all wait for signals to be confirmed even if this means giving up a few extra points of profit in the market. This system of signal validation is at the heart of the impressive success rates achieved in trading with Ichimoku.
- **Wait for the current candlestick to close** in the time frame studied, especially in the lower ones.

Contrary to other trading techniques, Ichimoku will make you enter the market later but with a greater likelihood of success. It is a relatively simple trading tool, keeping charts clear and free from a multitude of lines. Yet Ichimoku requires patience, and therefore waiting, much like the country in which it was developed: Japan.

5

ADVANCED TECHNIQUES

The trading system with Ichimoku presented in the previous chapters was based on the screening of three time frames regarding one's trading time horizon.

Thus, on an intraday basis, one will look at a 240-minute (H4) chart to get an overview of the market, an intermediate 60-minute (H1) chart to follow and manage the trade according to the strategy worked out, and finally a 15-minute chart to enter and exit the position.

A short-term trader (below 30 minutes) will need a 15-minute chart for a complete view of the market, a 5-minute chart to establish the trading strategy and a 1-minute chart to manage the trade.

Through four examples, I will now describe a more complete system still based on three time frames but by mixing two of them on a single chart.

1. DAX: 15-minute TF/60-minute projection (H1)

A correction is on the way, with a red candlestick testing the Kijun level below the Lagging Span. The latter bounced back on this support.

Chart 5.1: H4

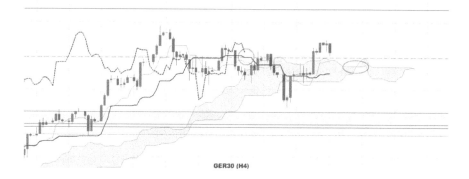

GER30 (H4)

Finally, the Lagging Span breaks below its Kijun and prices enter the cloud and find the Tenkan as support. The Lagging Span bounces back above its Kijun. The bearish signal is thus invalidated.

Chart 5.2: H4

GER30 (H4)

Let's take a closer look at this movement on shorter time frames: H1 and 15-minute charts.

On this 60-minute time frame, we clearly understand why the blue candlestick seen on the H4 chart can't go further up: prices are hampered by the H1 Kijun (green circle). This Kijun level thus appears to be the level to be watched closely for future price actions.

Chart 5.3: H1

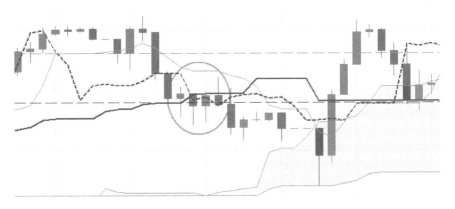

Now, we get back to the current prices on a smaller time frame (15-minute) while keeping this H1 view on the same chart.

The H1 time frame is represented with a green line for the Kijun and a green cloud. Immediately, we see the double support below the Lagging Span with the SSB of the 15-minute cloud and the H1 Kijun (green line).

Chart 5.4: 15-minute chart/projection H1

Prices got out of the cloud on the downside and broke the Hı Kijun. The third red candlestick reached the level of the Kijun Hı of the 15-minute Lagging span with its shadow. This candlestick closed on the level of the 15-minute Kijun (left) after a test of the 60-minute Kijun.

With this kind of double time frame analysis, it's easier to see the interaction between major lines such as the Lagging Span and the Kijun through different time frames, which will be more difficult to evaluate on separate screens.

This halted price action followed by a blue candlestick that invalidates the fall by breaking above the Hı Kijun is represented by the blue Doji in the green circle seen on chart 5.3.

Chart 5.5: 15-minute chart/projection H1

Then the 15-minute Lagging Span gets back to the top of its cloud (SSA) and prices stop on the SSB resistance and the Tenkan.

Chart 5.6: 15-minute chart/projection H1

Prices resume the fall with the H1 Kijun as first target which is strongly violated down to the SSB level. The 15-minute Lagging Span crosses back its H1 Kijun and tests its SSB (chart 5.7).

Chart 5.7: 15-minute chart/projection H1

GER30 (m15)

Each time a strong level is reached, prices stop and rebound. The 15-minute Lagging Span gets back above its H1 Kijun. A test of the break of the H1 Kijun by prices is expected.

Chart 5.8: 15-minute chart/projection H1

GER30 (m15)

That's exactly what happens. The important point to notice here is the move of the 15-minute Lagging Span on the H1 Kijun which acts as strong support. The candlesticks' shadows tell us that the Lagging Span tried several times to break this Kijun without success on close of the candles. Prices keep rising towards the H1 Kijun.

Chart 5.9: 15-minute chart/projection H1

GER30 (m15)

Price action above the H1 Kijun corresponds to the shadow of the fourth candlestick in the green circle (chart 5.3). If one only looks at an H1 chart, one only sees a Tenkan as resistance. Whereas on this chart (5.10) it is a Kijun on the same level as an SSB which acts as resistance. The information given is that it's a strong resistance.

Chart 5.10: 15-minute chart/projection H1

GER30 (m15)

Then, a short position could be entered when prices break the H1 Kijun once more. But while the Lagging Span is below its cloud, the H1 Kijun holds the fall.

So, we will have to wait before selling for prices to break down the trend line and for the Lagging Span to cross its H1 Kijun. But we have to keep in mind that the 15-minute SSB is on the same level as the H1 SSB on the far left of the chart. It is thus a strong support.

The red dotted line on the left is the H1 Lagging Span. In the following examples, we will see that it will give strong information while interacting with lines on shorter time frames. Here, it doesn't give any useful information. We will take notice of this line only when it will be close to 15-minute prices.

From this example, one has to remember that the most important line to look at for a validation of price action is the Lagging Span.

And the projection of a different and relevant time frame on the one used for the trade management enables a more complete view of the forces at play in the market. In the case above, the 15-minute Lagging Span encounters a strong obstacle with the H1 Kijun strengthened by the 15-minute SSB.

2. GBPUSD: 5-minute time frame/15-minute projection

In this example, prices try to confirm a reversal by crossing the cloud.

Even though the Lagging Span validates price action with a breakout of its Kijun, the upside trend struggles to carry on. Prices fall back into the cloud.

Chart 5.11: Daily chart

GBP/USD (D1)

The breakout of the Tenkan is a bearish alert but prices are hampered in their progression by the double support with the double level of SSB. If they happen to cross this threshold, the next target would be the Kijun.

We can consider two strategies:

- If the support holds, prices will exit the cloud on the upside and resume the bullish trend. A buy signal will be given.
- If prices breakdown this support, a sell position will be entered with the Kijun as target.

Let's look at shorter time frames.

Chart 5.12: H1

GBP/USD (H1)

The preceding upside move was well under way with the Lagging Span reaching the top of the cloud which acted as resistance. So, prices fell strongly and the Lagging Span got out of its cloud. The bullish corrective move is shown by the shadow on the daily candle.

Chart 5.13: H1

GBP/USD (H1)

Prices keep rising and cross the Tenkan level, a first step to invalidate the previous downtrend.

Let's study this movement on a shorter time frame looking at a 5-minute chart.

The 15-minute projection is represented by a green line for the Kijun and red dashed line for the Lagging Span.

Chart 5.14: 5-minute TF/15-minute projected

GBP/USD (m5)

At one glance, we can see that this move encounters significant resistances:

- Prices are capped by the 15-minute Kijun on the same level as the 5-minute SSB – it is a strong resistance.

- The 5-minute Lagging Span is hindered by the 5-minute Kijun and the 15-minute Kijun just above. But take notice of a twist in the 15-minute cloud above this double resistance. It is a bullish opening.
- On the left side, the 15-minute Lagging Span is neutral in its cloud and below the resistance composed of the 5-minute cloud around the 15-minute Kijun.

A good opportunity occurs here as a breakout of these strong resistances would give a strong price impulse on the upside.

Chart 5.15: 5-minute TF/15-minute projected

GBP/USD (m5)

The breakout considered happens in chart 5.15: prices cross this strong level and enter the 15-minute cloud, and the Lagging Span **breaks through its two Kijun**.

When both the Lagging Span and prices cross the same level, it's a valuable signal for a strong price action to follow.

Note here that the 15-minute Lagging Span (red dotted line) is useless.

Chart 5.16: 5-minute TF/15-minute projected

GBP/USD (m5)

Prices test with success the breakout of the Kijun + SSB and keep rising up to the next level, which is the 5-minute Kijun on the left. This is at the same level as the SSB that stops the 5-minute Lagging Span and the top of the 15-minute cloud (SSA) on the right.

The 5-minute Lagging Span crossed the 15-minute cloud twist and was stopped by the 5-minute twist.

The 15-minute Lagging Span broke its own Kijun in the middle of the 5-minute cloud and is stopped by the 5-minute Kijun. Prices are just above and could act as resistance to the progress of current prices.

On chart 5.17 we can see the end of this bullish price action with the 15-minute Lagging Span that is unable to break through its prices (green rectangle).

Chart 5.17: 5-minute TF/15-minute projected

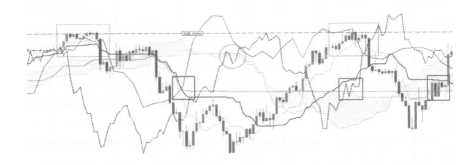

On the left green rectangle, the 15-minute Lagging Span (red) didn't manage to cross its 5-minute prices. And when it got between two candlesticks, it fell strongly after (see the big red candlestick on the right green rectangle).

The 5-minute Lagging Span (green circle) finally managed to cross the twist and was blocked by the 15-minute SSB level.

The display of two time frames on the same screen allows a better understanding of the interaction between lines from different time frames. At the beginning of the price movement, we are only interested by the 5-minute Lagging Span and the validation it could give on this specific time frame whereas the end of this rise is given by the 15-minute Lagging Span.

Likewise, one can perfectly see the high significance of the 15-minute Kijun with the two Lagging Span, reflecting the price action on the right-hand side of the chart (red rectangles): prices are negotiating a key area around this Kijun on the bottom of the 5-minute cloud and in the 15-minute cloud twist. This corresponds to the 15-minute Lagging Span crossing the 5-minute Tenkan and the 15-minute and 5-minute Kijun mingled. Finally, the 5-minute Lagging Span hesitates around the 15-minute Kijun mixed with the 5-minute SSB and is hindered twice by the 15-minute SSB as resistance.

One can immediately understand that it's highly recommended not to enter a position at this moment but to wait for the exit of the two Lagging Span and prices out of their respective clouds in order to validate the bullish resumption.

Although this sort of reading appears a little bit complicated at first sight, one gets rapidly used to it as soon as one masters perfectly the importance of each line of the system. The confluence of major lines such as SSB and Kijun are spotted rapidly and easily regardless of the time frame studied. Then looking at the position and movement of the two Lagging Span in relation to these strong levels enables you to build a powerful trading strategy.

3. DAX: 1-minute time frame

Now let's study a very short time frame.

Chart 5.18: H1

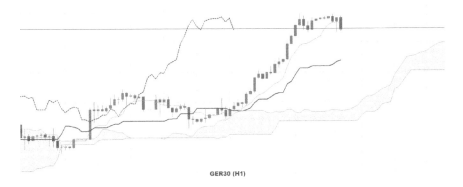

GER30 (H1)

First it is necessary to get an overview of the situation by looking at a long time frame. In chart 5.18, we clearly see that prices have been bullish for a while and they seem to halt this trend by making a top. The blue 'hanging man' candlestick gave a first signal that the uptrend could be over by breaking the Tenkan, invalidated on close. The current red candlestick gives a new bearish signal.

Chart 5.19: 15-minute

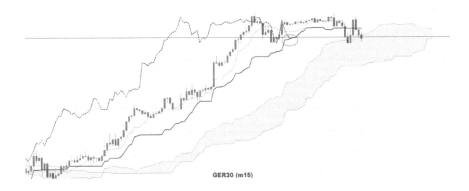

GER30 (m15)

On a shorter time frame, prices entered the cloud before getting back above the Kijun (downtrend invalidation) and then below again. The two blue candlesticks are the shadow of the H1 candlestick seen on chart 5.18. The Lagging Span has to break its Kijun in order to confirm the downside price action.

Chart 5.20: 5-minute TF/15-minute projection

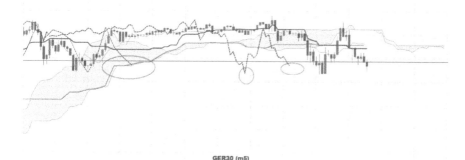

GER30 (m5)

On the 5-minute chart, chart 5.20, the 15-minute time frame is projected. On the left side, we can still visualise the Lagging Span (red dotted line) and its Kijun (green) as support but with more information: the 15-minute Kijun is strengthened by the 5-minute SSB (cloud bottom).

Likewise, one can see that the 5-minute Lagging Span tested twice the 15-minute cloud top which acts as strong support – this is the explanation for why prices don't resume their fall towards the cloud bottom.

Finally, a quadruple resistance level is taking place above prices with the 5-minute Kijun strengthened by the 15-minute Kijun on the same level as the 5-minute SSB and the Tenkan in between.

Chart 5.21: 1-minute TF/15-minute projection

GER30 (m1)

On chart 5.21, we get down to a 1-minute time frame to fine-tune the 5-minute price action seen in chart 5.20.

The quadruple resistance represented by the 15-minute Kijun (green line) appears to be in the middle of the 1-minute cloud. We can't see the 15-minute Lagging Span as it is situated too far on the left at 26 periods × 15 minutes = 390 × 1-minute candlesticks backwards.

Prices didn't reach the resistance level (two Kijun + SSB) because the 1-minute Lagging Span is stuck in its cloud (equilibrium). Thus, prices resume the downtrend through the 15-minute cloud.

Chart 5.22: 1-minute TF/5-minute projection

GER30 (m1)

Still on the 1-minute chart but with a 5-minute projection: we cannot see prices falling through a cloud, which is an important point.

The 5-minute Kijun is on top of the 1-minute SSB. So, if prices happen to break out the trend line and the 1-minute Kijun just above, the SSB/Kijun level will act as strong resistance.

Note that the 5-minute cloud is useless as it is too far from prices.

When you study a very short time frame chart, you only look for immediate information that is relevant for the next 5 or 15 minutes maximum. In the case above, any resistance above the 1-minute Kijun is useless as the market needs first to cross this line in order to reverse the downtrend and validate any upside movement. So, it will be better to look for any relevant support as a potential target.

So, the time frame projected will not be necessarily the closest from the one displayed. One will look for the most relevant, such as the 15-minute time frame in the example above. Sometimes, a H4 time frame will be projected on a 5-minute time frame because at that moment prices would possibly reach a strong H4 level, or are very close to it or are trying to break it. One will need to see how, on a short-term period, prices are working out this level so as to better evaluate the potential or direction of the movement that will follow the breakout.

This way of reading a chart is the fundamental contribution of Ichimoku to technical analysis.

The 15-minute and H4 time frames are the most relevant and give the better and stronger signals. Thus, they would often be chosen to appear as the projected time frame.

Furthermore, this kind of reading would be very useful on very short-term trading, especially when one wants to trade economic data releases. Because of a strong volatility, it will be very useful to project a higher time frame, such as H4 or H1, on a 1-minute trading screen. One needs to be both on a very short-term time frame to manage the position and see a much higher time frame to find out the price target and define a good technical stop-loss.

4. GBPUSD: multi-time frames

In the previous examples, I explained how to switch from a single time frame to a chart with two different time frames and how to find the time frame to be projected.

The following examples will show that sometimes one may also project different time frames on different basic time frames.

Chart 5.23: GBPUSD H1

GBP/USD (H1)

First, in chart 5.23, prices gave a sell signal by breaking down the Kijun. The question is whether it is only a pullback to test the breakout or is there any chance of an invalidation of this bearish move. For the latter, the Lagging Span and prices have to get back above their respective Kijun.

Chart 5.24: GBPUSD M15/H1 projected

GBP/USD (m15)

On a shorter time frame but keeping the H1 view as projection (green), prices are facing a double resistance: H1 Kijun + 15-minute Kijun. The 15-minute Lagging Span tries to break its H1 Kijun but finds resistance just above with the 15-minute cloud. And notice that the H1 Lagging Span (red dotted line) on the far left side of the chart is stuck both by the 15-minute cloud and the 15-minute Lagging Span. Thus, resistances on the upside are manifold and strong.

Chart 5.25: GBPUSD M5/H1 projected

GBP/USD (m5)

On a shorter time frame (5-minute) but still with the H1 projection, we can see that prices are working out their 5-minute Kijun after having tested the H1 Kijun. The 5-minute Lagging Span is moving around the H1 Kijun.

Chart 5.26: GBPUSD M1/H1 projected

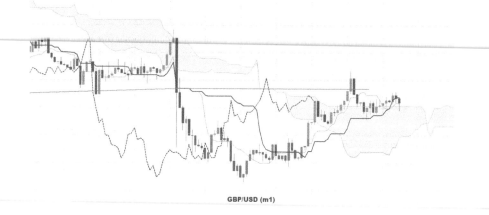

GBP/USD (m1)

At last on the shortest time frame (1-minute), prices' upside movement is well supported by the 1-minute Kijun and the market finds a strong support with the 1-minute thick cloud below. The 1-minute Lagging Span gets back in its cloud.

Remember that we try to determine whether prices will resume their fall or invalidate the sell signal given on the H1 time frame. By observing this latter chart, one clearly sees that prices tested the H1 Kijun with only one 1-minute candlestick and remain below it. It seems that the bearish movement initiated by the breakout of the H1 Kijun would resume. But the thick 1-minute cloud acts currently as strong support so it's a breakout test and not an invalidation of a bearish movement to come.

Chart 5.27: GBPUSD M1/H1 projected

GBP/USD (m1)

So, we keep this screen and observe the rest of the price action: the 1-minute Kijun still acts as strong support and prices resume their bullish move. They even manage to break again the H1 Kijun as the same time as the 1-minute Lagging Span.

Chart 5.28: GBPUSD M5/H1 projected

GBP/USD (m5)

Let's study the same movement on the 5-minute time frame: prices found a strong support with the 5-minute Kijun which happens to be on the same level as the 1-minute SSB (top of the cloud).

Chart 5.29: GBPUSD M1/H1 projected

GBP/USD (m1)

Back on the 1-minute chart: prices failed twice to break the H1 Kijun. The 1-minute Lagging Span remains below it. The explanation for this inability to continue rising comes from the trend line which hampered the price action.

Chart 5.30: GBPUSD M1/H1 projected

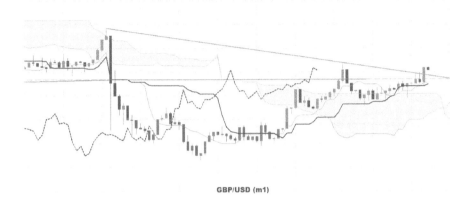

GBP/USD (m1)

With the 1-minute Kijun still acting as support, prices get both through the trend line and the H1 Kijun on close of the candlestick. The breakout test is in progress. But note that in order to validate a potential upside movement, the Lagging Span must also cross this trend line.

Chart 5.31: GBPUSD M1/M5 projected

GBP/USD (m1)

Now that the H1 Kijun key level has been broken, it is more interesting to switch on another projected time frame such as the 5-minute. Here the Lagging Span is stuck between the 5-minute Kijun and the trend line while prices are free to rise. So the Lagging Span doesn't confirm yet the upside trend.

Note that the 5-minute Kijun and the 1-minute SSB are on the same level. They will make a strong support above the twist close by.

Chart 5.32: GBPUSD M1/M5 projected

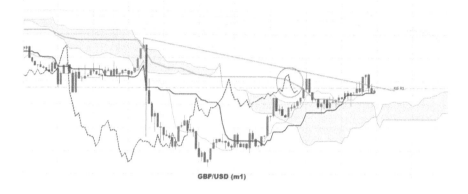

GBP/USD (m1)

The breakout of the trend line is invalidated and prices fall back towards the double support Kijun + Tenkan. The 1-minute Lagging Span also invalidates the bullish price action by getting back below its 5-minute Kijun without breaking above the trend line.

Chart 5.33: GBPUSD M1/M5 projected

GBP/USD (m1)

Prices try once again to break the trend line and the Lagging Span breaks the 5-minute Kijun.

Chart 5.34: GBPUSD M1/M5 projected

It's a failure – prices remain below the trend line and the Lagging Span doesn't cross the 5-minute Kijun on close.

Note that the twist below prices is of no interest as it is obstructed by the 1-minute and 5-minute Kijuns. Prices have barely a chance to get through it.

Chart 5.35: GBPUSD M1/M5 projected

The 1-minute Kijun is very strong and prices try once again to break the trend line. But this time the Lagging Span gets well above the 5-minute Kijun and crosses its prices. Its next resistance is still the trend line.

Chart 5.36: GBPUSD M1/M5 projected

GBP/USD (m1)

At last prices validate the breakout of this trend line + the H1 Kijun (dashed green line) on close. They are now free to rise. But note that another resistance is near with a second plateau of the 5-minute Kijun which crosses the trend line just above the Lagging Span.

Chart 5.37: GBPUSD M1/M5 projected

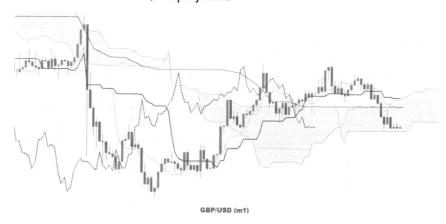

GBP/USD (m1)

Finally, prices didn't confirm the upside movement with a lower high below the second 5-minute Kijun level seen on chart 5.36 and they give a double sell signal by breaking both the 1-minute and 5-minute Kijuns. This bearish impulse stops on the bottom of the cloud (SSB).

A breakout of this last support would resume the downtrend initiated on H1.

Chart 5.38: GBPUSD 15-minute

GBP/USD (m15)

Now let's get back to a higher time frame so as to have an overview of this movement.

On this 15-minute chart, you can clearly see why prices couldn't move higher with the Kijun as resistance. The trend is still bearish and the upside movement was only a correction with three blue candlesticks.

Chart 5.39: GBPUSD M1/M15 projected

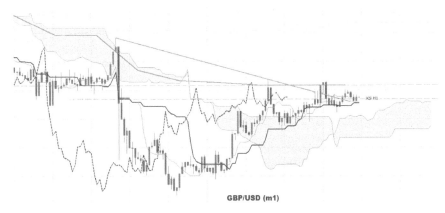

GBP/USD (m1)

Let's have a look at the same 1-minute price action but with a 15-minute projection. Prices are stuck between the 1-minute and 15-minute Kijun. It's neutral on a short-term basis.

The attempt to break the 15-minute Kijun seen on chart 5.38 appears more clearly here: it happens only with a 1-minute candle. Thus, it can be considered as a market excess.

Chart 5.40: GBPUSD M1/M15 projected

GBP/USD (m1)

Finally, prices fall following the 1-minute Kijun breakout. The Lagging Span gets through its own Kijun and confirms this downside movement.

Looking back at chart 5.37, one can see that the 1-minute Kijun is situated between the 15-minute Kijun as resistance and the 5-minute Kijun as support. It therefore appears to be a strong key level for the direction of the trend.

Chart 5.41: GBPUSD M15

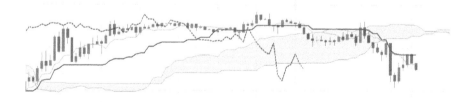

GBP/USD (m15)

Prices seem to resume the downtrend with the break of the Tenkan. The Lagging Span confirms by getting out of its cloud. The three blue candlesticks correction is over and one could consider selling the pair.

Chart 5.42: GBPUSD M5/M15 projected

GBP/USD (m5)

Fine-tuning the previous chart by getting on a shorter time frame, one can see that the 15-minute Kijun is on the same level as the 5-minute SSB (top of the cloud) on the right-hand side of the chart. So, it is a strong resistance. And the bearish price action is confirmed with the breakout of the 5-minute Kijun, validating the signal given on 15-minute chart 5.41.

Chart 5.43: GBPUSD M1/M5 projected

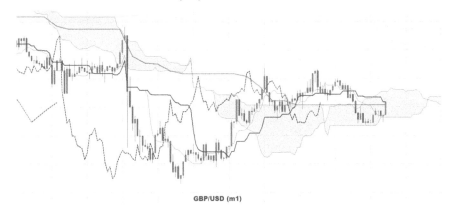

GBP/USD (m1)

But looking again to the 1-minute chart, prices found strong support with the SSB and reversed the trend by rising back up to the double resistance of the 1-minute + 5-minute Kijuns. The Lagging Span gets through its double resistance of 1-minute SSB + 5-minute Kijun. The fall is halted.

Chart 5.44: GBPUSD M5/M15 projected

GBP/USD (m5)

The price action seen on chart 5.43 is represented by the Doji on the 5-minute time frame.

Chart 5.45: GBPUSD M1/M5 projected

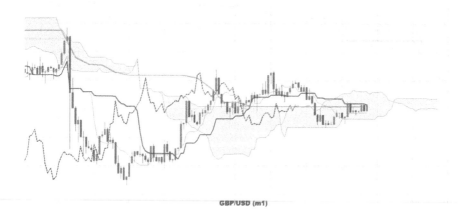

GBP/USD (m1)

Here is the Doji split into 1-minute candles. Prices are revolving around the 5-minute Kijun which they can't manage to break because of the 1-minute Kijun acting as resistance. However the Lagging Span breaks its 5-minute Kijun + the top of the cloud for the third time.

Chart 5.46: GBPUSD M1/M5 projected

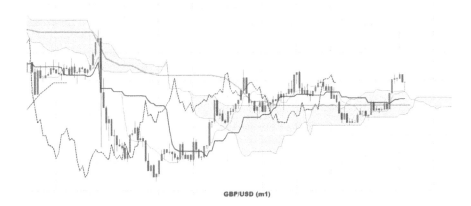

GBP/USD (m1)

Finally, prices created a thrust outside the 1-minute cloud by breaking the two Kijuns. The Lagging Span also breaks its two Kijuns and is now free to move upward.

The next resistance to watch for (it could be set as a price target) is the thin 5-minute cloud.

One can consider once again to buy the market as prices get back to the old 5-minute Kijun level already tested.

Chart 5.47: GBPUSD M5/M15 projected

GBP/USD (m5)

Switching to higher time frames, one can clearly see the thin 5-minute cloud (blue) but the upward movement which seems easy on the previous chart (5.46) could be hindered by the 15-minute Kijun (green) on the same level as the 5-minute SSB to the right, an old resistance which already blocked prices (chart 5.44).

On this chart the 15-minute Lagging Span is introduced (red dotted line to the left). It rises inside its cloud and has more room on the upside. It tells us that the price resistance should give up.

Chart 5.48: GBPUSD M5/M15 projected

GBP/USD (m5)

That's exactly what happened. Prices manage to get through the thin 5-minute cloud and keep rising up to the 15-minute cloud.

The 5-minute Lagging Span breaks its prices and the Tenkan + Kijun resistance confirming the price action. It rises up to its 5-minute cloud which acts as resistance. And the 15-minute Lagging Span (red) crosses its prices and its Tenkan and is finally hampered by the 5-minute Kijun.

A buy position could have been entered when prices tested the breakout of the 15-minute Kijun in line with the 5-minute SSB. The target could not be set higher as the level where prices stopped was a confluence of resistance on different time frames, both for prices and for the two Lagging Span. Prices couldn't move higher right now.

Chart 5.49: GBPUSD M5/M15 projected

GBP/USD (m5)

This strong confluence of different levels acts as strong resistance. Prices rapidly fall back towards the last resistance which is now a support. The Lagging span has been repelled by its 5-minute cloud twist inside the 15-minute cloud.

In conclusion to this example, one can easily understand why shuffling through several time frames with different time frame projections could be a major advantage for very short-term trading. One is thus able to better visualise various supports and resistances and define their strength through major confluences.

Whereas the projected time frame was close to the time frame displayed, it may be sometimes more useful to project a much higher time frame, especially when one wants to trade the release of economic statistics.

Chart 5.50: GBPUSD M15/H4 projected – statistics release

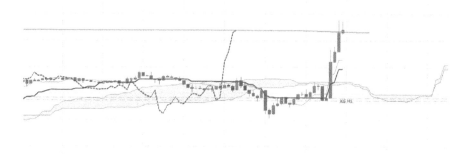

GBP/USD (m15)

Chart 5.50 is the continuation of the price action observed in the previous example.

Prices were hampered by the 15-minute cloud and fell back towards the Kijun. The thrust upward happens following a US statistical issue. The key level to be watched for defining a target was on an H4 time frame, quite far from the 15-minute one used for the trade (it could have even been a 5-minute or 1-minute trading chart). The H4 Kijun was reached with three blue candlesticks. The current blue one should turn red on close and thus indicate a correction of this strong move to follow.

This wide gap between the trading time frame and the one projected is necessary in such a case to take into account the strong volatility.

Thus, these examples show how convenient it is to use a system of time frame projection. Note that only the cloud and Kijun are projected, and sometimes the Lagging Span when the time frame projected is close to the trading time frame.

As explained in previous chapters, in order to establish a trading strategy, three different time frames need to be looked at. One could say that it could be handy to project the three time frames needed on a single chart. I do not recommend such a system as it will be difficult to read and excerpt the most relevant information.

Now let's study more in detail the importance of the Lagging Span.

5. Various examples: the Lagging Span

A. GBPNZD: Weekly/H1/H4

Chart 5.51: GBPNZD Weekly

GBP/NZD (W1)

On this weekly chart, the market is bearish below the cloud. This downside price action has been confirmed by the Lagging Span which broke its own Kijun and a key level (Kijun + SSB) just below.

A pullback is in progress so as to test this breakout in order to validate the bearish trend.

Chart 5.52: GBPNZD H1/H4 projected

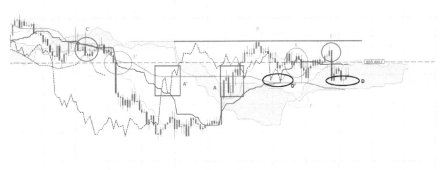

GBP/NZD (H1)

On the hourly chart (5.52), in the red rectangle A, the market tries to get out of the H1 cloud (blue) and is hampered by the H4 Kijun. The corresponding Lagging Span (blue dotted line) in rectangle A' wavers between the two Kijuns.

Once the H4 Kijun is broken prices keep going upward to the H1 SSB level (B) and don't reach the H4 thin cloud, which could have been set as a target. Then the market falls down to the H4 Kijun, crossing the top of the H1 cloud which acts as support. Prices move up again until the H4 cloud (C) making a lower high.

At this point the H4 Lagging Span (blue circle C') showed that this upward price action was doomed to failure as it was blocked by too many resistances: prices + H1 SSB + H4 SSB + two Kijuns and the H1 Tenkan, all inside the two interlinked clouds.

The following violent decline from C stops in the middle of the H1 cloud (D) which is none other than the H1 Lagging Span (D'), which bounced on the double support H1 + H4 Kijuns. But a strong resistance (E) would halt the Lagging Span rebound which is on the same level as a strong resistance for the H4 Lagging Span (E').

So, there is more probability for the market to resume a downtrend than to rise. As soon as it breaks the H4 Kijun doubled with the H1 SSB, the H1 Lagging Span would probably go through the twist (F) and confirm the bearish trend. On the other end the H4 Lagging Span would be totally to fall.

B. GBPNZD: 5-minute/15-minute projected

Chart 5.53: GBPNZD 5-minute/15-minute projected

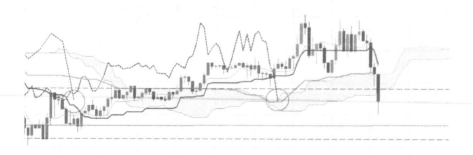

On this chart an interesting phenomenon happens with the two Lagging Span hindered by their opposite Kijun: the 5-minute Lagging Span finds a strong support with the 15-minute Kijun doubled by the SSB and at the same time, the 15-minute Lagging Span would be stopped by the 5-minute Kijun.

Despite a violent drop both support levels hold.

C. GBPNZD: H1/H4 projected

Chart 5.54: GBPNZD H1/H4 projected

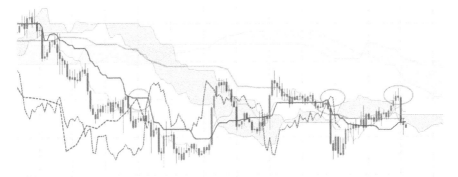

In the two green circles on the right side of chart 5.54, the market is free to rise as both prices and the H1 Lagging Span have managed to break their resistance on the upside.

But this movement is halted by the H4 Lagging Span (left side of the chart) as it encountered the H1 Kijun.

In conclusion one must always pay attention to the Lagging Span and their interaction with the Kijuns and SSB from different time frames, which can only be visualised with a time frame projection such as those presented in this chapter.

When looking at simple and separate time frames, it is impossible to get this kind of view which is most relevant in trading.

Now that one knows perfectly how to analyse a chart with Ichimoku and trade ensuing strategies, let's see how Ichimoku could be a significant contribution with other classical tools of analysis.

PART 3

ICHIMOKU AND OTHER INDICATORS

Introduction

Now, for Westerners who are impatient and less Zen, it's possible to add other indicators or classical chartist patterns. These patterns will have even more probability of being validated when they correspond with Ichimoku levels.

In the following chapters we will see how Ichimoku can then be used to complement analysis performed through other techniques, so as to avoid wrong signals and to avoid entering a trade too early, which is doomed to failure.

The point of view taken here is the contribution of Ichimoku to other technical tools and not the opposite. Indeed, Ichimoku being a complete system of analysis, adding any other indicator would only blur the simplicity of analysis and unnecessarily complicate the decision-making process.

So most traders look at moving averages – simple or exponential – to define entry/exit levels or trend reversal. But the main disadvantage is that one has to set the right parameter to each market studied and to each time frame. A 100 moving average does not have the same meaning on H1 or 1-minute charts, for example.

Ichimoku presents two lines which are very close in their reading to moving averages: the Tenkan and the Kijun, but their parameters are fixed whatever the time frame or market. Thus, adding a moving average on the chart studied will bring nothing more in the understanding of the market action.

Never forget that the more indicators or lines one puts on his chart, the more potential support/resistance appear to impede the price action, the more the analysis will be complicated and the less the trader will be confident in his strategy if he ever happens to enter the market.

Personally, the only technical tool that I find very useful and often unavoidable in the short term is trend lines systematically taking into account a candlestick shadow extremity which represents a price negotiated by the market. That's why drawing trend lines on the Lagging Span doesn't make sense as this line is set from the close of the candlestick, thus ignoring the shadow.

We will see that in addition to the traditional breakout of a trend line by prices, it will be more than relevant when the Lagging Span gets very close to it. It thus will be a last validation signal when all other support/resistance are useless. Many breakouts would be invalidated by the Lagging Span unable to cross the same trend line later on. This is another filter for wrong signals.

Let's see this action through examples:

Chart III.1: Trend line

A. Above (chart III.1), prices failed twice to break above the SSB as a trend line provided resistance just above (circle in chart)

Similarly, in the chart below (chart III.2), the trend line follows the Kijun very closely. The Lagging Span still must break below this line to validate recent bearish price action. The trend line may be an obstacle to such a technical break.

Chart III.2: Trend line and Kijun

B. Now let's see the major interaction between a trend line and the Lagging Span

On chart III.3, after having crossed the cloud twist and broken the trend line at the same time, the bearish trend induced by these signals fails to gain momentum. The reason for this is the Lagging Span, which is rebounding off the trend line while prices consolidate within a range. The Lagging Span finally passes up through the cloud twist, allowing prices to break above the Tenkan. Prices may now fail to follow through with this rebound at the SSB/Kijun/ trend line triple resistance.

Chart III.3: Trend line and Lagging Span

Chart III.4: Breakout of the trend line

On chart III.4, prices are bullish after a breakout of the trend line. A Doji appears and prices are set to halt their rise in 'the middle of nowhere'. But the Lagging Span gives the explanation: it doesn't manage to get through the medium-term (MT) and short-term (ST) trend lines and gets stuck below these two levels. Prices may fall towards the trend line or even to the Tenkan below. As the Lagging Span is free to move downside, a test of its SSB could be possible.

On this chart, one can also notice that when prices got through the thin cloud and were stopped by the MT trend line, it was no other than the Lagging Span which remained in its cloud. It would not have been wise to enter a long position on the breakout of the cloud by prices. Adding the ST trend line reinforced the probability of the Lagging Span staying inside its own cloud.

This example perfectly highlights the importance of a trend line breakout being validated by the Lagging Span. Moreover, the concordance between trend lines and Ichimoku levels is clearly apparent.

Chart III.5: Daily

On chart III.5 prices broke the trend line and are currently testing this break by a pullback. The SSB should act now as support. On the other side the Lagging Span finds a resistance with its prices.

Looking at a shorter time frame (H4, chart III.6), prices tested this trend line for the last five candlesticks and the Lagging Span couldn't manage to get through it. But the SSB seems to be a strong support.

Chart III.6: H4

This kind of movement tells one to wait for the Lagging Span to confirm the price breakout by breaking the trend line. The pullback of prices on both the trend line and SSB appears clearly and is most relevant. It was wise to be cautious with this breakout.

Chart III.7: Non-valid breakout

Here is a new example of a double trend line. Prices clearly give a bullish signal having crossed the two trend lines and the cloud twist. But the Lagging Span is hampered by the long-term (LT) trend line, the latter being on the same level as the SSB on the right side of the chart.

In such cases, it is not recommended to enter a position as long as the Lagging Span has not crossed the two trend lines. Note that the shortest one is doubling the cloud SSA. Thus, when the Lagging Span will get through this level, it would be a strong validation of the uptrend.

Therefore, the most important point a trader must always keep in mind is to leave a trend line drawn on his chart even though it becomes useless for prices. One must wait until the Lagging Span has also got through.

C. The following two examples present another kind of trend line: Andrew's pitchfork

Chart III.8: Prices and Andrew's pitchfork

Prices first stopped on the SSB before getting out of the cloud and were stopped again by a second level of an SSB and the pitchfork median line. These corresponding levels gave good information regarding the probability for prices to resume the downtrend and break the cloud bottom on the left.

Chart III.9: Lagging Span and Andrew's pitchfork

On this chart (III.9) prices are far below their pitchfork top line but the Lagging Span revolves around the median line unable to break it. But just below, the double level of Fibonacci 0.618 ratio should act as strong support and make the Lagging Span get through the median line. Prices would thus move upward so as to reach the upper line of the pitchfork, which could act as resistance. In a trading view, this level could be set as a take profit.

Chart III.10: Andrew's pitchfork

Here is the continuation of the movement: the Lagging Span crossed the median with prices testing the upper line for the first time. Then after a pullback of the

Lagging Span on the median, prices tested once again the upper line but are hampered by the Kijun which fell down.

Trend lines are the only additional lines that I consider with Ichimoku because they're the only tool that provides useful information to the indicator. Having tried almost everything in different time frames, all the other additional technical tools are simply 'icing on the cake' and will do more to confuse traders than to provide them with a more refined understanding of the market traded.

I make the assumption that 'too much information kills information and leads to misinformation'; this is also true regarding economic and political news, as much as it is for the number of technical indicators viewed in a given chart.

The more charts are free of lines and indicators and provide a clear understanding of price movements, the simpler the analysis will be. **In trading, simplicity is a must.**

6

FIBONACCI

Human beings are creatures of habit. They like to live in a comfort zone that protects them and encourages them to constantly act the same way. This type of behaviour is found in the form of patterns that repeat with the same results.

As markets reflect the psychology of players, these patterns of behaviour are reflected in chart patterns in technical analysis.

Leonardo Fibonacci of Pisa, a mathematician of the thirteenth century, studied the natural repetition of patterns in nature by asking himself a question: how many pairs of rabbits in a pen can be produced in a year from a single pair of rabbits, if each pair gives birth to a new pair each month counting from the second month? The answer is 144. The genius of this question lies in the formulation of the answer:

1,1,2,3,5,8,13,21,34,55,89, and 144.

This series of numbers became called the Fibonacci sequence, where any number in the sequence is the sum of the two preceding numbers.

An interesting feature is that as one moves along the sequence, the ratio of consecutive numbers in the sequence approaches the golden ratio of 1.618. This golden ratio and its inverse, 0.618, are the primary ratios of Fibonacci chart analysis from which all the other ratios are derived.

Thus, Fibonacci ratios are present throughout nature, defining the natural progression of growth and decay. In other words, they represent evolution in the form of cycles.

It is through the study of ratios that one can understand the concepts of proportion, symmetry, harmony and rhythm. Market prices will rise and fall bounded by certain ratios derived from previous price action.

We will therefore look for patterns in the price with impulsive movements, either bullish or bearish, to which these ratios can be applied in order to understand better the current price trajectory.

The following table lists the major ratios, derived from the golden ratio, used in Fibonacci analysis.

1 − **0.618** = 0.382	**0.618** − 0.382 = 0.236
0.618 × **0.618** = 0.382	**0.618** × 0.382= 0.236
√**0.618** = 0.786	**1.618** × **1.618** = 2.618
√**1.618** = 1.272	**1.618** × 2.618 = 4.236
With **0.618** being the reciprocal of **1.618**	

The use of these ratios on a chart allows the trader to identify key levels of support and resistance, and thus to define trading strategies.

To do this, it will look for convergence zones of these ratios by applying two different types of relationships: retracement and extension.

Retracement

This is calculated from the lowest point to the highest point in a bullish movement and the reverse in a downward direction. It is always less than 100% and is used to determine a price target in a correction.

Chart 6.1: Retracements

The 78.6% level is considered the maximum level for a correction. In case of a close beyond this level, the correction will continue in this trend to reach a new trough (or peak).

Extension

While retracements concern price falls from a recent high (or rises from a recent trough), extensions concern (swing) movements that are in the same direction.

Only levels above 0.618 are considered. The objective here is to obtain a price target in a fundamental trend following an intermediate correction.

Chart 6.2: Extension

Retracements combined with extensions will give narrow areas for price targets. They can also give a possible level for turnaround of a correction or even a change of trend.

Chart 6.3: Retracements and extensions combined

If an extension is not close to a retracement, it will only be considered as an intermediate level of support or resistance.

An extension of 100% is not sufficient in itself, it must be confirmed by a retracement to a key level.

In the example above, a large convergence zone appeared on the retracement level of 0.618 and the extension of 1.272. Prices marked this latter resistance by three candlesticks with shadows. The movement then moves towards the next level (0.786/1.618).

If you now look at the Ichimoku on the same chart, further information appears that is particularly relevant.

Chart 6.4: Trade example, DAX (5 min)

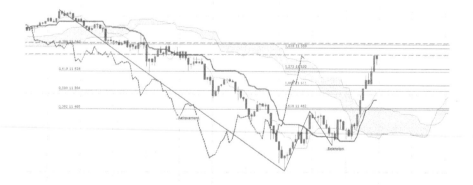

Thus, the first resistance identified by the ratio 0.618/1.272 lies exactly in the extension of a Kijun plateau of the previous bearish movement. However, it should be remembered that these previous levels of Kijun remain valid for future movements. A good example here.

Then the bullish recovery stalls before reaching the level of 1.618. Similarly, it is a Kijun plateau of bearish movement that is influential here.

Chart 6.5: DAX (5 min)

We can see in the above chart that the price corrected by returning to the previous level crossed, which is at the same level as the Tenkan.

The corrective movement seems to be greater than expected. The breakdown of the Tenkan tells us that the bullish movement is possibly over. A retracement between the points (B) and (C) and an extension ABC (see chart 6.6) will therefore be in place again. This gives us bearish levels of convergence on which prices could halt or even bounce back in order to rise to the previously expected level of 1.618.

Chart 6.6: DAX (5 min)

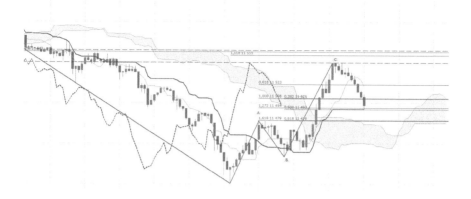

Three levels are clearly identified: the one at 1.00/0.382, 1.272/0.50 and that at 1.618/0.618. The latter seems to be the primary level to consider as they are the two most important ratios of Fibonacci. It also corresponds to an Ichimoku support in the presence of a cloud top (SSB) under prices in the extension of an SSB on the right. The attractive power of an SSB being high, it is a level not to be neglected.

Chart 6.7: DAX (5 min)

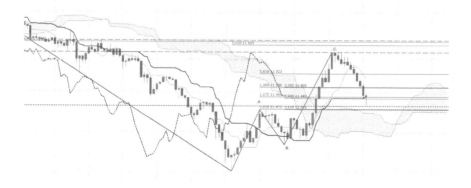

Remember that the Kijun corresponds to a 50% retracement of the movement which is corrected. This is indeed the case here, and it is not surprising that a Doji is formed at this level, indicating that the price will not go lower. And the extreme level envisaged was almost reached by the Doji shadow that stopped on the Ichimoku level of the SSB (blue dotted line).

Here is the final chart of this movement.

Chart 6.8: DAX (5 min)

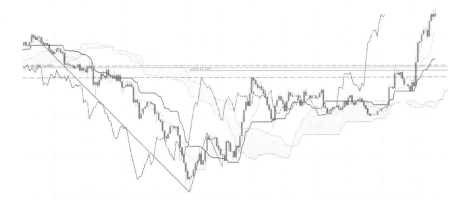

After a long consolidation following the closing of the market, prices resumed their bullish progression from the opening of the market the next day and went to reach the level of 1.618.

In this example, it would have been quite possible to be satisfied with only the retracements and extensions of Fibonacci to manage a position. But the addition of Ichimoku makes it possible to validate these levels and to be alert when prices are close to a target defined by a ratio.

When one looks closely at the main bullish movement, one can see that since the exit of the cloud each candlestick ends on the same level as an Ichimoku line. Indeed, it can be seen that prices mark the levels given by Ichimoku more clearly than those of Fibonacci. The clearest example is this last level of 1.618 which is not reached (not even a shadow); it is blocked by the SSB on the left.

Chart 6.9: DAX (5 min)

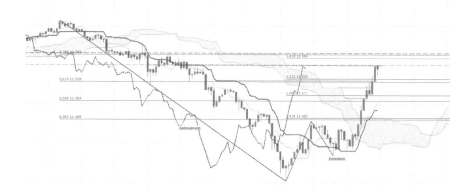

Similarly, it is Ichimoku that signals the end of the correction with the Kijun, which plays its supporting role while maintaining the uptrend intact while prices close above it. It is the SSB level touched by prices that would have taken us out of a position, selling from the start of the shadow, thus indicating that the Fibonacci ratio of 1.618/0.618 would not be reached.

In the following example, prices did not go lower than the support area defined by the retracement ratio of 0.618 and the extension ratio of 1.414. One might have expected that the market would look for an extension to 1.618, which is a strong ratio. But this is not the case, not even on a shadow.

Chart 6.10: GBPJPY (day)

The addition of the Ichimoku makes it easier to understand why.

Chart 6.11: GBPJPY (day)

With Ichimoku we can see that it is the Lagging Span that refuses to exit its cloud and to validate the fall initiated by prices.

A zone of possible targets is envisaged with just a reading of the Ichimoku, considering the two plateaus of Kijun and the SSB on the left. And that corresponds to the 1.618 extension. This level was therefore relevant.

But the SSB, on the same level as the 0.618 and 1.414, provided support for the Lagging Span and therefore for prices.

Chart 6.12: GBPJPY (daily)

The extra information given by Ichimoku is that this double level of Fibonacci ratios was strong and therefore that the next ratio would not be reached.

For a trader who works mainly with Fibonacci ratios, a projection of Ichimoku will be useful to validate the relevance of certain levels and to determine target and stop-loss levels.

By contrast, a trader working only with Ichimoku can use Fibonacci retracements and extensions when he has few points of reference, especially during long trend movements.

The shift to longer time frames can be difficult (many trading platforms do not offer time frames greater than monthly). And even quarterly or yearly charts may not help.

Chart 6.13: DAX (yearly, log scale)

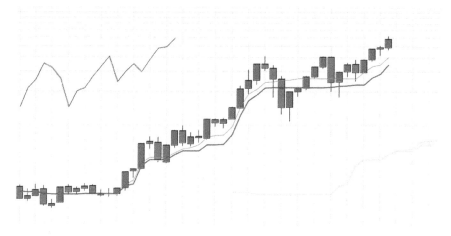

The yearly chart, 6.13, confirms the upward trend but offers no target levels.

Chart 6.14: DAX (quarterly, log scale)

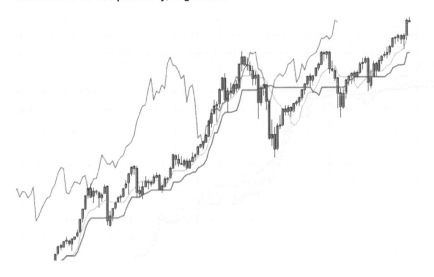

And the same on a quarterly chart.

In these cases, Ichimoku gives only supports that will tell us to take a position but no target levels.

But the trader wants to know where he is heading!

On the monthly chart, 6.15, prices are largely above the Tenkan and the Kijun, the cloud is far away and the Lagging Span has no near obstacles. The configuration is identical to those of the two longer time frames.

Chart 6.15: DAX (monthly)

The only possibility is to use the extensions of Fibonacci and to find the most relevant areas of convergence in order to define target levels.

In this particular case, a first zone (1.618, 0.618, 1.272) which should have acted as resistance was crossed by the third blue candlestick. The target that seems most relevant afterwards is on levels 0.618, 2.000, 0.886.

It is here that Ichimoku as a trend indicator has its limits, since it can no longer offer target levels. It can only alert us if the trend begins to weaken with a breakdown of the Tenkan, or if it reverses following a break of the Kijun. On the other hand, it remains useful to read the possible levels during a correction and it will give validations of counter-trend position when prices break down through the Tenkan.

PART 4

THE ART OF DISCIPLINED TRADING

Trading the financial market can be exciting, but it is not necessarily quite as simple as some advertisements portray it. Reading some books and articles on the internet, or even paying for expensive trading lessons and software, will not be sufficient to make you rich overnight. So, why not? Why is the failure rate so high among new traders despite their intelligence and enthusiasm?

The answer is simple.

For many people, to succeed in life involves making enough money to live life as one wants. And some believe that trading will enable them to do this. This is not impossible, but successful trading (low-risk and efficient) is based on a paradox: **financial gain cannot be the motor of trading but its consequence**. The initial motivation that drives one to want to trade must not interfere with the proper business of trading.

Why?

By removing the primary goal of money from his mind, the trader understands the markets as a logical exercise, and if he is right then profits will follow. By separating the analysis from consideration of the p/l account, in other words thinking in terms of points and not money, the trader is better able to objectively deal with the market.

It is a matter of deliberately forgetting why you are trading (to make money), to allow the brain to **focus on signals that the market actually gives rather than signals that you want to see**. The desire for profit makes us see opportunities where they don't exist and therefore becomes a source of error. This affects all traders from beginners to experienced: we are all human whereby emotion can affect our judgement. The trading battle plays out less on screens than in our heads, between the subconscious and the decision-making process.

This is the field of neuroeconomics, a new science that tries to explain the psychology of market players through neural mechanisms, which has shown how, despite all our reasoning and all the information available to us, mistakes are always possible. Experience indicates that any threat to a human triggers primary emotional reflexes that analytical intelligence must counteract in order to respond appropriately. Reasoned activity occurs when unconscious activity encounters an insoluble problem. But reasoned activity is not infallible.

Indeed, most decisions are made in a context of risk, and we have a natural dislike of risk. This applies as much in the management of our daily life as in more dangerous situations. Trading falls between these two extremes and uses the same emotional stimuli of our brain that we must learn to manage in order to achieve the best financial choices.

We must therefore first get to know our emotions in order to develop our decision-making process.

I. Know your emotions

Managing the psychological aspect of trading represents 80% of the work. Even with the best technical analysis and the best decision-making tools, the trader can never be a winner if he cannot control his emotional state. Indeed, the emotional part of our intelligence is not only dominating but also reacts more quickly than the analytic part.

1). Fear

This is the most important emotion: the fear of financial loss. A brain examined by MRI in a situation of financial loss shows that the affected area is the same as that stimulated by the presence of deadly danger. It is the expression of the fundamental instinct of preservation on which our speed of reaction depends. This is why severe or incoherent market conditions provoke irrational and therefore often negative reactions.

We are especially scared **before getting into a trade**. For example, the fear of losing money can encourage us to increase the number of technical indicators on a screen, thus providing a false impression of better understanding the market. But by considering too much information, we can lose time: the market moves forward and obliges us to run behind it instead of looking ahead. The psychological pressure will force us to enter into a position so as not to miss an opportunity, even if all the signals are not green. This impulsive behaviour generates more losses than gains.

Subsequently, fear is also present **when the position is open**. For example, the fear of losing the paper gains if the market turns against us. We are hyper-sensitive to the slightest signal of a possible market pause or reverse and may close the position. But this impulse towards safety can result in frustration, and even anger, when the trader views his modest gains as the market goes on to hit his original target. The error is not due to a lack of skill but a lack of **confidence**.

2). Hope

When a trade does not go as planned, a trader can hope that the market will eventually go his way, and as a result of such thinking he may even increase his position size. The strong sensation of loss masks the reality of the signals which invalidate the initial analysis. **To prove that one is right** is an emotion that constitutes an important psychological trap.

Hope also manifests itself in the **expectation** of an opportunity. Patience can be undermined by inaction, which makes one want to act on the slightest suspicion of a signal partly to justify having spent hours without doing anything.

3). Euphoria

A sense of euphoria can follow a succession of gains, which can lead to a sense of ease, or even invincibility. This can lead to impaired judgement and the rapid loss of previous gains. Which then opens the way to anger and losses in an infernal spiral.

4). Anger

After several disappointments, anger can push us into the market with the idea of making up our losses. This is the same kind of excessive activity where we enter the market on the slightest signal, persuaded that this is *the* movement that will allow us to recover the previous losses. Again, the result is usually disastrous, sometimes resulting in panic.

5). Panic

Panic is the acute feeling of no longer understanding the market. Overwhelmed by losses, we are paralysed by perplexity and impotence. In this case, two options are available to us: to act at all costs (necessarily in an irrational way, because one is no longer able to reason), or to do nothing and get out.

But in our society the idea of losing is often associated with **shame**. And the psychological pain can be worse than a physical pain because it takes longer to heal. Every time a trader finds himself in a similar situation to one where he previously lost, the pain can be easily recalled. This financial, but above all psychological, damage to one's ego leads to doubts about oneself.

6). Doubt

Doubt is the main obstacle to decision-making. In the markets there are two type of doubt. The first doubt is the questioning of our system, which causes it to lose its reliability and function as guide. The second type of doubt is hesitation, which prevents us from acting at the right moment.

Taking a position therefore requires a certain form of **courage**. The trader is tested. And the test can lead to success if he strictly respects his system, or to failure if his emotions are poorly controlled.

These emotions which can lead us to behaviours contrary to our interest are unavoidable since they are part of us. They motivate reason, but they must not overstep their rightful place. Trading thus involves two aspects of the brain: **reason**, which develops a strategy for taking a position in the market, and **emotion**, which activates the implementation of the strategy.

The goal is therefore to learn to deal with one's emotions. It is only then that we can associate ourselves positively with the emotions. It is not a question of ignoring them but of recognising their existence in order to let them go in favour of a frame of mind of calm and determination.

II. Building your decision-making process

The trader is constantly confronted with choices to be made to deal with an unknown future. And these choices involve a decision process sensitive to the emotional state. However, it is possible to reduce this sensitivity by developing good habits.

1). Take your time

It is not necessary to get up at dawn to better understand the markets. Further, price fluctuations at market open don't necessarily give a good guide for price behaviour the rest of the day. As such, settling down in front of the screen after the market has opened can avoid many distractions and be more relaxing.

Success lies in the timing of the trade and therefore in patience. It is necessary to wait until the market gives a correct signal according to our system. As long as this signal is not present, the trader must remain inactive.

2). Take your bearings

Before looking for trading opportunities, the trader must work to understand the prevailing mood in the market. This involves developing feelings for the market – a process of observing without necessarily wishing to interpret everything. Listening to the market makes sense since it is aggregate translation of the psychology of the actors involved. This is how one becomes in tune with the market and able to perceive when the moment to act approaches.

Knowledge and technical know-how are essential, but the emotional state of mind of a trader at the time of action is of paramount importance. So, it is a matter of framing the involuntary actions that we have identified through rational mechanisms. In other words, what we want is **action based on solid discipline**. This will preserve the integrity of the analysis even in situations of unexpected market action.

If we dismiss emotions from trading does that mean that traders should become like robots? No. In practice, it is a matter of giving oneself the means to **remain calm** by learning to control one's mind. One must stay Zen in front of the screen, and be detached by imagining one is an external observer.

3). Train your mind

This is the basis of the technique: the trader must work his mind as a sportsman trains his body.

The first step is that of **introspection**. Learning to know oneself as an individual: what is your degree of resistance to stress, what are your reactions to unforeseen events, or your ability to concentrate? And knowing yourself as an actor in the market: why are you in the market and what do you expect from the market? It is by determining the weak and strong facets of *your trader personality* that you will be able to have confidence in your work.

The second stage is to build a theoretical model of our activity. It aims to optimise our strengths and minimise our weaknesses. Being fully aware of these we can set realistic performance targets. This will give meaning to our actions without thinking in monetary terms (as we saw at the beginning of the chapter). And then it is necessary to assess the probability of achieving our ambitions: what are the potential obstacles and what are the means at our disposal to achieve our objectives?

This stage of reflection exists to allow us to quickly start trading in the best conditions, and thereby avoiding a large part of the trial and error that punctuates the practice of many traders.

The last step is to formalise this reflection into **a strict and immutable framework of skills**. The trading mission then becomes as smooth as possible. Although it sounds daunting, defining a rigorous application of strategies results in a pleasing confidence and calmness and it's profitable! This is developed through technical analysis combined with optimal risk management to control emotions.

III. In action

Imagine yourself facing your screen, the market situation is neutral and your trade progresses in accordance with your strategy. Suddenly, external information disturbs this balance and provokes from you a reaction to try to re-establish stability.

1. The first reaction is emotional: are you in danger (the survival instinct)? Here, the question is more likely to be: is the strategy at risk? What do I feel: fear, anger, anxiety? Do I have to react quickly or do I have time for reflection?

2. The second reaction involves analysis: the brain processes the disruptive information in order to define several possible response options from which the final decision will lead to regain stability.

3. The last reaction will be the application of this decision.

This sequence, which describes the successive states of a trader in front of a screen, can equally describe the markets themselves. Prices show a stable or neutral trend, something happens that disrupts the balance, market players begin by contagiously reacting to manage their positions and then, after analysis and reflection, adjustments are made to recover equilibrium. The market will most often then resume its initial trend.

By imposing order on an apparent mess, trading rules rationalise our uncertainties and our changing perceptions of reality by putting ourselves into a process of intervention. This process is an intellectual scheme that allows the trader to disconnect his actions from emotional fluctuations. As a neutral witness to the turbulence, the trader can feel the market as it appears and make the most objective decisions possible.

How to set up the process

Analyse the market

The best traders use naked charts, that is to say they look at prices without any addition of lines or indicators on their screen. This stripped-max makes it possible to feel the market perfectly. "Simplicity is the ultimate sophistication," said Leonardo da Vinci, but it is not easy to achieve this and usually requires several years of experience.

In the meantime, there is a wide range of analysis tools available on trading platforms. The first step is to select the most relevant, and especially those that fit your type of analysis. There is no one miraculous tool: you must simply find the one that most clearly helps you understand the market. To have too many tools will be confusing: the brain, interpreting the information of each one in an independent way, will take more time to synthesise them (not counting those that contradict each other).

Hence the interest in an indicator like Ichimoku, which is self-sufficient and which instantaneously gives a comprehensive view.

Evaluation

An intuitive reading of the market, through experience or using technical analysis tools, is necessary to anticipate price movements. It is imperative to understand what is going on in order to have conviction and therefore optimal confidence when entering the position.

From the synthesis of his observations, the trader establishes his strategy for the market: the entry point, the price target and the stop level. The size of the position will be determined by the risk/reward ratio. All the trader has to do is wait for the timing to trigger his scenario.

Managing the position

Managing a position requires concentration and self-confidence. It is necessary to be in the market, to follow the movement of prices, to live it through to the final objective. I like to compare this stage at the heart of trading to the activity of an archer: one must be the tension of the arc (strategy), the trajectory of the arrow (the market movement), and the target (the goal). And for that, no doubt is possible as soon as the bow is released. The trader monitors his position with full confidence because he automatically follows his trading plan: he has already planned responses to the vagaries of the price, the alternatives, and the options to be implemented if things deviate from the original hypothesis.

Win, but also lose

Any trader, even experienced ones, will lose from time to time despite his knowledge and his method because he operates in a world where chaos reigns. It is natural to make mistakes, but this also gives opportunities to learn. These losses help traders correct bad habits and to persevere even in difficult times. Knowing how to recognise ourselves and react correctly in certain situations helps us to face future potential threats. **To learn is to survive.**

We should look therefore to take advantage of these errors and not excuse them by generally blaming the market.

The attitude of the good trader is obviously to try to minimise these losses. To do this, we must approach the market without prejudice, and make ourselves open to what the market can offer. It is through hard work, flexibility of mind and experience that a trader acquires a critical mass of information that will allow him to develop an **intuition**. An intuition being an immediate perception of reality, a fundamental trust in what he sees that enables him to remain above successes or failures that merely confirm what he already knew.

To summarise:

- **Never stop learning.** It is necessary to have an open and curious mind in order to gather as much information as possible about the market.
- From the learning will come **knowledge** which will offer **intuition** and which will lead to a better understanding of the market.
- Thus, a strong **confidence** is built.
- This confidence is secured by a **system** that responds automatically to profit opportunities in the market.
- This method of trading control must take into account the key lessons of behavioural finance, it must be as simple as possible in its construction, precise, and above all adapted to the trader's personality.

IV. Conclusion

Motivation, passion and energy are essential to succeed. It is important not to be discouraged by the difficulty of trading and the money at stake.

We're not trying to get something from the market for nothing. It is through hard work and an open-mindedness that we will be able to grasp what the market offers us. We must be in tune with the market and feel when the conditions are favourable so as to have the emotional and physical impulse to seize it at the right time.

Intuition grows from a mass of information accumulated over time. It leads to quick and accurate judgements when trading rules are simple. The best decisions are thus based on the double capacity of the brain: intuition and analysis, reasoning and feeling.

Only a real apprenticeship and constant technical and mental training allow the application of a method adapted to the psycho-financial profile of the trader. The resulting emotional detachment offers a better sense of the reality of the market.

This attitude of total objectivity while in the market can only be achieved if we disregard the primary purpose of our action, namely to earn money. This must be concealed and thought only as a result of our trading. Money should only be a means of measuring the success of the rigorous application of our strategy.

Trading is not just buying and selling to make money. It is also learning to know oneself and to overcome one's fears. The reward is the pleasure of being able to master the art of trading itself.

The ideal trader profile

A good trader is one who knows how to build an effective strategy based on his feelings of the market. He must be able to listen and understand what he truly sees in order to seize the best opportunities.

He must concentrate on the process of applying his method and not on the results.

Through his experience, he must be able to adjust his scenarios with alternative options in order to control the risk.

He must always be in the Present and not influenced by Past events or try to extrapolate to the Future. He must leave aside his errors and losses (from which he has learned the lessons) and concentrate only on the immediate actions of the market.

He must be in the market, to live it and experience it fully through complete emotional detachment.

A good trader is one who is continually learning, with the accumulation of knowledge of markets and technology. And he develops his emotional skills by concentrating on increasing his concentration and his insight.

The experienced trader is a lucid and scrupulous tactician who applies a disciplined strategy.

The behaviour of the ideal trader

- Know why you trade: what are the objectives and are they easily achievable? Are your financial resources sufficient?

- Always act according to your own judgement: establishing a reliable method in which you are confident means never being influenced by others.

- Be as systematic as possible.

- Never base trades on hope: everything must be analysed and calculated before entering the market.

- In case of doubt, remain outside the market. You must have total confidence in the reason that drives you to run a trade. This is imperative to best manage a position. If the analysis is proved wrong, exit.

- The decision to trade must be based on potential gains but also on possible losses.

- Always have several alternative options for achieving your strategy – a chess player always plans several moves ahead.

- Don't chase the market; let it come to you. Read the market without over-interpretation and wait for the signals that accord with your analysis and strategy. In other words: don't overtrade.

- Do not look for highs and lows, but wait for reversals and their confirmation to take the middle of the movement the strongest. The question to ask is: is the trend confirmed, and not: is the trend going to turn?

- Do not take all the reversals because some will be weak and unprofitable.

- Do not fight against the trend, but it is possible to play the corrections bearing in mind that one is temporarily against the fundamental direction.

- Always calculate the risk/reward ratio in order to optimise the size of your position and limit the extent of losses.

- A stop-loss must be technical, and the size of the position adapted to the expected loss.

- Cut losses (discipline) and do not stay in hope mode, thereby freeing yourself from the emotional weight of the loss and saving your capital.
- Do not always try to prove that you are right. The market is the Master of the Game.
- Allow profits to run while no exit signal is present.
- Prefer several small, low-risk trades to spread the risk.
- Prefer trades in a liquid market.
- Make a regular mental inventory of your progress: trading is an intellectual process.
- Always analyse your negative trades to learn the lessons, but also the positive trades to gain confidence in your abilities. Understanding yourself is paramount.
- Stop trading after a series of losses: do not lose confidence.
- Stop trading after a series of gains: avoid over-confidence.

Trading is **patience**, **discipline** and a **system** adapted to your psychological profile.

"Be patient and unemotional: there are periods when traders don't need to trade."

Typical trading plan

1. Choose the type of market, assets and the unit of time.
2. Assess the potential profit and the associated risk of loss.
3. Establish the position size according to money management and market sensitivity.
4. Define the entry point according to proven technical signals.
5. Plan the exit on technical points (e.g. support, resistance, retracement or extension of Fibonacci etc.).
6. Calculate the stop-loss, which must be both technical and financial.
7. Determine entry conditions (e.g. volatility, break tests etc.).

These rules must be established and be consistent with the trader's emotional personality.

Principles of money management

- Divide your capital into n equal shares and use only 1/n of this capital per trade.
- Do not execute too many transactions in the same period: this is a rule of capital preservation.
- Do not allow profits to turn into losses by moving the stop-loss to ensure gains.
- Trade in active and liquid markets.
- Diversify the risk.
- Do not close positions impatiently or enter due to lack of action.
- Never cancel a stop-loss.
- Treat each trade separately.
- Do not change your mind without a good reason.
- Do not follow the advice of others.
- If in doubt, exit the market.
- Consider the importance of timing in trend changes.

CONCLUSION

It is true that too much information kills information. This applies equally to economic and political news and also to the number of indicators we have on our screens.

The more the screen is kept clean the better it can show market movements, and the analysis can be kept simple. And in trading, simplicity is of paramount importance.

As a reminder, Ichimoku Kinko Hyo means 'see the balance of a graph at a glance'. How can one have a quick and accurate view of the market if the screen is congested and each element must be analysed separately? Do not forget that Ichimoku is a complete analysis system that forms a whole. Generally, analysis will be longer if you add more indicators to your screen, and this is not the goal when you want to use Ichimoku.

In conclusion, I would simply say:

1. If you want to keep with your current charting method, consider also looking at the Ichimoku chart of the same market to act as a verification of the key levels and strategy.

2. If you are not satisfied with your current charting method, then consider a radical change by re-learning how to read a chart using only Ichimoku. This requires a bit of hard work and willingness to forget previous habits, but it's worth it.

3. If you are new to trading then it is easy, you only need to put Ichimoku on the screen and you can learn to read the chart in a pure way.

For me, the second case applied. I believe it is better to follow one complete method (i.e. Ichimoku) than continually incorporating further charting tools that just act to complicate the analysis process. As a result, my success rate today is significantly above average.

And, finally, if you want to succeed at trading I believe the keys to success are: simplicity, rigour and patience.

www.ingramcontent.com/pod-product-compliance
Ingram Content Group UK Ltd.
Pitfield, Milton Keynes, MK11 3LW, UK
UKHW020725120225
454980UK00002B/18

9 780857 196156